Becoming Coach Shaw

Mrs. Nkonoki-Ward,   12/4/14

I give all the honor and
glory to God.

Becoming Coach Shaw: How I Learned to Run My Own Race

Darwin F. Shaw with Kerry L. Beckford

ISBN: 978-1500437626

Cover design and book design by Ciar McGhee

Author photograph by Russell Kimball

To contact Darwin F. Shaw:
becomingcoachshaw@gmail.com

To contact Kerry L. Beckford:
www.kerrybeckford.com

To Porcia, Myia, Garrett and Julian

Always remember to run your own race

PREFACE

When you come from a household in the inner city and your mother has four kids by the time she is 18 years old, you know that your life will not be easy. Although we had a father, he was a hustler and pimp who never lived with us. The odds were stacked against my sister, brothers, and me. I knew that it was going to be difficult to get ahead in life because of the hand that I was dealt.

I could have ended up in prison. I could have sold drugs or joined a gang. I could have died before my life got started. There would be times of struggle, unbelievable loss, and some very bad decisions. But God had a different plan. He put people in my life who helped when they could—family, friends, pastors, teachers, coaches and many others who lived in the community. I was lucky to have people who saw something in me that—with the right amount of nurturing— could be amazing.

As a teacher and coach for the past 29 years in the city that I grew up in, I look at the way God put me in the position to help people. I talk with students every day. They share with me some of their concerns and secrets that they have never shared with anyone, even members of their own families. I know what they are dealing with because I see myself in them. I also see what tremendous potential they have to do incredible things with their lives. I've learned that life really is like a relay race: when you reach for the baton ahead of you, you are trusting that someone will be there to pass it along. I see kids every day who need someone to be there when they are reaching for that baton.

I am proof that anyone who may be lost does not have to stay lost.

This book is about how I learned to run my own race. Life is full of people who *need* help but life is also full of people who *want* to help. One does not have to be an All-American, Hall of Famer or a legend to make an impact in someone's life. The most phenomenal, life-changing influences come from average, everyday people. Like I said, I don't have all the answers but it is time for me to pay it forward. I hope that by telling my story, you will learn that life is a series of hills and valleys and that very good people are already in your corner to help you to achieve your dreams.

Darwin F. Shaw
June 2014

CHAPTER ONE

PLEASE, THANK YOU, AND YOU'RE WELCOME

For the first few years of my life, everything I needed and wanted was in Scranton, Pennsylvania. It's the city where I was born, where my grandparents and cousins and friends lived. It would be many years before I knew that Scranton was not the biggest city in the world, that other cities had churches and schools and playgrounds and variety stores just like Scranton. My boyhood would have been complete if I could be seven years old forever. Then I could spend all of my time playing kickball and football with my friends and my cousins, or just running up and down the street. Up Adams Avenue, around the corner to Pine Street, across N. Washington Avenue, and back. Careful not to throw the ball near Mr. Smith's car and don't trample on Mrs. Moody's tiny lawn. In the house before the street lights come on. Eating the sweet potato pie my grandmother saved just for me.

By the time I was in the second grade, life could not have been better. We lived on Lee Court, one of the main streets in the Central City section of Scranton. We all went to James Madison Elementary School. It was a three-story brick building located on Quincy Avenue and was only a few blocks from my house. The school was made of red and beige bricks and looked to me like a castle. It had wide hallways with hardwood floors and marble tiles in the bathrooms. Our school did not have a kitchen, so they did not serve any hot lunches. Adults liked to make a big deal out of the fact that we went to a school named after the 4th president of the United States. None of that impressed me at the time. When you're seven years old you care more about lunch and recess than anything else.

One of the best things about second grade was that I got to walk home from school every day for lunch. We entertained ourselves the entire way home. Dinky, who was like the ring leader among us, told joke after joke. I liked that he had a nickname because I had one, too: everyone called me Bubby. My mother's friend once said that I looked so happy that I was bubbly. Pretty soon, bubbly became "Bubby." When an adult called me Darwin, it was because they didn't know my nickname or because I was in trouble.

Sometimes we would play games on the way home, like seeing who could kick a rock from the school to our house or we would play catch the football without dropping it.

My cousin, Myron, always seemed to win both games all of the time. He hated losing so many times he would cheat by saying he caught the ball even when he dropped it. We argued one minute then forgot about the argument the next minute, as children often do.

Moms always made a nice lunch for my older brother, Jeffrey, my younger brother, Early, and Dawn, who was the oldest and our only sister. Lunch was either grilled cheese sandwiches or soup. It wasn't fancy but it was what my single mother could afford to feed four children.

One fall day in 1967, I was walking home from school for lunch with my sister and brothers and some of my friends. It was starting to rain, not too hard but enough so that it made me want to walk faster. My jacket was really light and I knew if it rained a lot, my jacket would get soaked. I was pretty sure I would make it home before the rain got heavier.

While we were walking, fire trucks were going by us, their sirens piercing the air. "Fire! Fire!," we yelled. We tried to keep pace with the fire trucks but they moved too fast. A few people were looking out windows or stood on their front porches to see where the fire trucks were headed. The fire trucks were going in the direction of my church, which you had to pass before you reached my house. The closer we got to the church, we could see that the fire wasn't there but the crowd of people grew with each step I took.

As we entered Lee Court, we saw three fire trucks and more people standing around. My mother was one of those people standing outside. I thought this was strange because it was lunchtime and my mother was serious when it came to our meals. If we didn't eat our lunch on time, we would be late getting back to school. Standing next to Moms was her friend, Anita Jackson. They didn't have any coats or sweaters on and the rain started coming down harder. I ran to see why she and Miss Jackson were standing outside. Before I could reach them, my friend Elmo said, "Your house is on fire!"

Flames shot out of the windows and black smoke made the gray sky darker. I remember thinking that it was strange that the firefighters were using so much water. It was raining hard by then and I hoped that the rain would put the fire out and that we would have our lunch and get back to school. That was not going to happen.

Everyone in my family was standing together crying. I was upset but didn't cry too much. I was trying to find out if anyone got Mike out of the house before it caught on fire. Mike was our pet turtle. We couldn't have cats or dogs but my mother thought a turtle would be a suitable first pet for four busy kids. There wasn't any chance that Mike would get lost but, just in case, my mother used bright pink fingernail polish to paint his name on his shell.

I knew that Mike was in trouble because no one had him outside. As the tears started streaming down my face my mom grabbed me and I wrapped myself up in her arms. I said, "Mike is in there and he is going to die because nobody is bringing him outside!" The firefighters did what they could but the house was destroyed and Mike was lost in the fire.

That night, we stayed with my mother's parents, Francis and Madeline Williams, who lived up the street from us. Grandma's house was my favorite place in the world because we never went hungry and she loved to bake. The aroma in the house always smelled good, like cinnamon, nutmeg, and vanilla. My grandparents' house was not big but there was enough room for us.

Although we were shaken by the fire, my grandmother remained calm. She loved the Lord and took church seriously. We talked all the time and she never failed to say the right thing to say to me. The night of the fire, as I was getting ready for bed, my grandmother knew I was not only upset but angry. "Why did God let our house burn down? Why did God take Mike to heaven?" I demanded to know. I thought Grandma would be mad at me because she constantly told me that I should be grateful to God. My house was gone and Mike was, too. There wasn't a lot of room for gratitude.

Grandma sat by the side of the bed that I shared with my brothers for the first of what would be many nights at her house. "Bubby," she said softly, "this may be hard for you to understand now but you were given life for a reason. From now on, you need to find out what that reason is." I didn't know it then, I couldn't know it then, but what my grandmother said that night was the beginning of a life I could never imagine.

After the fire, it took a long time for me to be happy. Why did Mike die? Why did the house burn down? I went to church with my grandmother all the time and we were learning that God always protected us. But that couldn't be true in my case. My grandmother could tell how sad I was and she often told me that I could have died in that fire. "You should be grateful that the Lord spared your life, Bubby," she said. I was trying but it was hard.

We lived with my grandparents for a few months after the fire. If you lived in my grandmother's house, you had to go to church. Well, almost everyone. My grandfather wasn't really the church going kind. He thought it was fine that Grandma went to church but he wasn't that religious and only went once in a while. He worked so hard at his job as a porter with the Erie-Lackawanna Railroad and he liked to be home when he could. My mother didn't go to church, either. She partied on Saturday nights and was hardly ever in the mood to go to church on Sunday morning.

Our church was Bethel A.M.E. Church on N. Washington Avenue and our pastor was Reverend Fletcher Burgette. It was a small brick building with two wooden doors in front. Grandma joined Bethel when she was 17 and it soon became her world. She was the supervisor of the Sunday school, which meant we had to attend Sunday school at 9:00am and then regular church at service 10:45. The church was a few blocks from her house and it wasn't unusual to find her at the church throughout the week.

If my grandmother was not at Bethel, she was usually at home. Grandma never drove a car, drank, or smoked. My grandmother had four friends who kept her company: Mrs. Haynes, Mrs. Caddy, Mrs. Kearney, and Rev. Burgette's wife, Mrs. Burgette. And my grandmother never, ever went anywhere on her own and—especially when it came to her own house—you knew she would be in the company of people she loved and respected.

One day my grandmother asked me to walk to church with her and when we got there she asked me to open the front door of the church for her. As I proceeded to open the heavy door, I heard Rev. Burgette say, "I'll get that for you, Mat." The adults called my grandmother Mat, which was short for Madeline. Younger people called her Miss Mat. I think Rev. Burgette was probably the only other person who was at Bethel more than my grandmother. He wasn't a tall man but he had a commanding presence. He wore glasses and was clean shaven. Like many ministers during that time, Rev. Burgette had another job. He was a chauffeur for the Casey family, who owned The Hotel Casey in Scranton. To me, he was Rev. Burgette.

When Rev. Burgette opened the door, I started to walk through it. My grandmother grabbed me by the shoulder and placed me behind her as she walked through the door that Rev. Burgette was holding open. After we both walked through she thanked the reverend and then looked at me as if I was supposed to say something, too.

"Is there something wrong with your voice?" she asked me.

"No," I said. I was getting the feeling that I was in trouble. But there was just the three of us. I didn't run into the church or yell or do anything of the things that would have made my grandmother angry with me. She took one step closer to me and exhaled slowly.

"Someone just did something for you, Bubby," she said as she glanced at Rev. Burgette. All this time the reverend was as still as a statue. He didn't have a mean look on his face, he never did. But I could tell that he was hanging on my grandmother's every word. Grandma was looking at me with eyes that meant business even though her voice was calm and steady.

"When someone does something for you, let them know that you like what they did by saying thank you."

My grandmother was a patient woman and she would make us stay just inside the church doors until I did what she asked. I turned toward Rev. Burgette and quietly said thank you. He extended his hand to me as if to say *"You're welcome."*

Every Sunday I looked forward to walking with my grandmother to church. When I walked with my grandmother, I acted like I was protecting her even though it was the other way around. I was spending more time with my grandmother since the fire and even though I loved staying with her, some days it was all I could do not to cry about losing our pet turtle and wondering how long we would be able to live in her small apartment. It was like my grandmother knew everything I was thinking and feeling and she took the time to make sure that I filled my time thinking of anything but the fire.

Most of my friends and cousins attended Sunday school and church. Many times we arrived early to help my grandmother to set up the classrooms for Sunday school. Sometimes we had to wash the tables, unfold the chairs, and then make sure that the books were on the tables for the Sunday school lesson. When Sunday school was over, we had to fold and stack the chairs. It was a busy job for us kids but at least there were snacks left on the counter in the kitchen for us to eat.

After Sunday school, a few of us went upstairs to pass out the weekly bulletin. The people who went to Bethel A.M.E. had jobs as maids, chauffeurs, and cooks. A lot of the men worked for the Erie-Lackawanna Railroad or took construction jobs where they could find them. But on Sunday mornings, they all dressed like kings and queens. The men had finely pressed suits and shiny shoes, and the women wore pretty dresses and fancy hats. My cousins and I were usually the first people they would see when they approached the front doors of the church. Passing out bulletins was serious business; if my grandmother found out we were clowning around, we would get in so much trouble that even the good

Rev. Burgette couldn't save us. So, we passed out bulletins and said a polite "You're welcome" to everyone who said thank you.

Sunday morning work seemed like a job to me because my grandmother used to give me and my brothers and sister 40 cents. That money was supposed to make its way to the collection trays during Rev. Burgette's service. Every now and then we would sneak to Matasses, a variety store around the corner from the church, and spend all of the money. We only did that when it was Grandma's time to sing in the choir. She had to go in another room upstairs to put on her robe with the other ladies and that's when we would sneak out and return before church got started. If she wasn't singing that day, my grandmother's eyes made sure every quarter, nickel, and dime went from our sweaty palms to the collection plate.

As I got older, thank you, please, and you're welcome became part of my daily language. Grandma would ask if I used any of those phrases throughout the day and I had to give her some examples of when I used them. Each time she asked me, I was ready to answer. Mrs. Caddie gave me lots of opportunities to use my grandmother's favorite words. Mrs. Caddie lived down the street and she usually needed help with something. I would stop over there unannounced before I went to my grandmother's house.

"Do you need me to get you anything from the store today, Mrs. Caddie?" I would ask.

"Why, Bubby, yes I do," Mrs. Caddie replied. "Could you go across the street to Frank's store and get me a newspaper or some cigarettes?"

After I returned with the paper, she would say thank you and give me a quarter. I would say thank you and go to Rev. Burgette's apartment, which was in the same building as my grandmother's. If I did something for Mrs. Burgette she would ask if I wanted freshly baked cookies or brownies.

"Yes, please, Mrs. Burgette. Thank you, Mrs. Burgette."

Running errands for people was getting to be worthwhile for a kid like me. Sometimes the reward came before the work. A lot of times Mrs. Burgette would leave a bag of cookies with my grandmother. Grandma would make me go upstairs to thank Mrs. Burgette for the cookies and see if she needed me to do anything for her or Rev. Burgette.

After church sometimes we would help some of grandma's friends take their belongings to their cars or just simply open the door for them. One day, Mr. Kearney, one of my grandmother's friends who played the organ for the church, needed help taking some things to his car. After I helped him he gave me a quarter and I said, "Thank you, Mr. Kearney." He replied, "You are welcome, young man." I showed my grandmother what he gave me and she said, "Sometimes you get rewarded like that when you are kind to people." The fire had taken away a lot but I was getting much more in return.

You may be going through something that seems hard to understand. Maybe you asked yourself, "Why am I here when nothing ever goes my way?" One answer is that life is not easy and that a lot of things do not make us happy. And when you are not happy, being courteous may be the last thing on your mind.

When you're a kid, it can be hard to recognize the importance of being courteous. The point is not the physical reward; it's how you feel when you've been kind to someone. Small acts of kindness let people know that you care about them, that you see them as valuable human beings. You can accomplish great things with these powerful words:

**Please, Thank You, and
You're Welcome**

CHAPTER TWO

THERE IS ALWAYS A PLAN
FOR YOUR LIFE

In the months after the fire, we managed to step into a normal routine: school and playing with our friends, running errands for Grandma and her friends on Saturdays and church on Sundays. I was usually hungry after church. Maybe it was because Rev. Burgette's sermons lasted forever or maybe it was because my Sundays started really early in the day. All I know is that I could have eaten the church bulletin but we could not leave Bethel A.M.E. until we said goodbye to every elder in the church. My grandmother was big on manners and we didn't rush her goodbyes.

When we finally got home from church, it was time for dinner. Even before the fire, we had Sunday dinner at

Grandma's. It felt normal to keep this tradition. Moms cooked for us before the fire but she only made enough for one meal. My grandmother cooked all the time. At her house, there was so much food for one meal, I found myself expecting extra people around the Sunday table. They were so different, my mother and grandmother. I often had to remind myself that they were related.

My grandmother never cooked on the Lord's Day, which is why she spent all day Saturday cooking and baking. With all of us living with her, I bet my grandmother was glad that she had a dining room. Grandma sat at one end of the table and—when he was home—my grandfather sat at the other end. His job as a porter for the railroad kept him away from home for weeks at a time. The Erie-Lackawanna Railroad ran passenger trains from New York City to Buffalo and Chicago. My grandfather worked on the most famous passenger train called the Phoebe Snow, which took mostly white families on their way to and from vacation. Air conditioned cars kept the sleeping quarters cool for the wealthy passengers and the dining rooms were as fine as any restaurant. The porters did everything from storing luggage to making beds, serving food, and shining shoes; anything to keep the passengers happy. The train stopped at the Lackawanna Train Station on Jefferson Avenue in Scranton to pick up or let off passengers. Sometimes my grandfather had less than an hour to run home to get new clothes before getting back to the train to work nonstop for a few more weeks. That's why it was a treat when my grandparents were home at the same time.

On Sundays, dinner was served promptly at 3:00pm. By then, my mother was ready to eat after partying the night before. She didn't go to church but respected my grandmother enough to eat Sunday dinner with us. The table was set with a tablecloth, Grandma's best plates, silverware, and drinking glasses. We had to wash our hands before we ate and never, ever ate a morsel until Grandma said grace. Only then could we dive in.

It was worth the wait. Give her two, maybe three ingredients and my grandmother made a feast. Roast beef. Fried chicken. Macaroni and cheese. Potato Salad. Candied Yams. Fried catfish. Greens. Homemade biscuits. And Kool Aid. Lots of Kool Aid. She told us to eat everything on our plates because some people in the world didn't have anything to eat. The one thing she cooked that I did not like was lima beans. I was happy that my grandmother made sure there was enough food for all of us, but I had a hard time being grateful for those lima beans. When she wasn't looking, I took a few at a time off my plate and stuffed them in my pocket. The minute I was excused from the table after dinner, I flushed those lima beans down the toilet.

Lucky for me, my grandmother never found out how I got rid of the lima beans. If she did, my punishment would have been no dessert. As much as my grandmother was a good cook, she was a fantastic baker. Sometimes she made cookies for dessert but every Sunday, her sweet potato pie was waiting in the kitchen. She baked the pies on Saturday in her tiny but well-used kitchen. She made the best pie crust in the world and the richest, smoothest sweet potato filling. I tried to make sure that I was in the kitchen when she was making the pie because she let me lick the spoon.

We were lucky to have my grandparents to lean on during that time. My father, Earl Shaw, lived in Scranton but he was not the type of man who was interested in being a father. He was a hustler and a pimp. Moms never talked about him and did not factor him into our lives. Sometimes we saw him hanging around but we knew better than to reach out to him to try to build some kind of relationship. It was just as well because he didn't try to be a father to us. Moms was the only parent we needed.

Eventually, Moms found us another apartment on Olive Street. It was right down the street from Grandma's house and I was able to spend as much time with her as I wanted.

Olive Street was a busy street in the city of Scranton. There were apartments, stores, and local businesses with names like Jack's Sweet Shop, Frank's Variety Store, Ben's Tailor Shop, and Tony's Barber Shop. When black folks came to town, they came to Adams Avenue and Olive Street.

There were two bars on our street, one on each corner: the Melrose and Mo's Bar. Our new apartment was on the second floor. Mo's was on the first floor. The bar was owned by Harold M. Wolfe, whose nickname was Mo. After a Friday and Saturday night of partying, the outside of our apartment was a mess from all of the trash. Sometimes my friends and I would help pick up the trash and Mr. Wolfe paid us about 50 cents, which we spent on candy at Frank's Variety Store.

My mother was a lot like her friends: single young women who tried to stay young even when kids and jobs made them more grown up than they wanted to be. It was the late 60s, when black was beginning to be really beautiful and Motown was turning out records every week. But Scranton was not Detroit and it definitely was not New York. It was just a small city where black folks like my mother tried to make a decent life from one weekend to the next.

Moms was the stay-at-home type, except on the weekends. She was a pretty woman with caramel colored skin who wore wigs and prided herself on dressing nice. She and her friends would go to the Melrose or Mo's on a regular basis. Every Friday and Saturday night, they would meet in our living room. Moms was the center of attention when she was playing hostess. She put us to bed before her friends came over but we could never sleep because they were too loud. They drank and laughed and teased each other while they smoked funny smelling cigarettes that weren't Marlboros or Winstons. They weren't telling any jokes and at the time I thought it must have been the music or the cigarettes or the liquor that made them laugh. My brothers and I would open the bedroom door just enough to see them dancing to the music playing on the record player even though the music from Mo's was loud enough to hear in our apartment. My mother made sure her music drowned out whatever was playing downstairs in the bar.

We watched them do that kind of partying all night long every Friday. On Saturdays, my mother stayed in the bed for most of the day resting up after a rough night. She wouldn't get up until early in the evening so that she could get ready to party again. By the time Sunday rolled around, going to church was the last thing on her mind.

My mother was pretty quiet unless she was with her friends. It's like some kind of switch turned on during the weekend and my mother was a different woman than the one who made us grilled cheese sandwiches for lunch.

Other than hanging out in those two bars, my mother had a good job working at the Topps factory, where they made

Bazooka bubble gum and other types of candy. It was the perfect place for Moms to work because she loved sugar. She would bring boxes of bubble gum home and my brothers and sister and I chewed bubble gum like they were vitamins.

My mother also loved to drive. She had a new Cutlass Supreme every other weekend. My close friends really thought we were well off because of the kinds of cars that she drove. The truth was that my mother also worked at a car wash and she rented cars from her boss. Every time she wanted a different car, all she had to do was ask.

Although I spent a lot of time down at my grandmother's house, I loved being around my mother because she was a funny lady. She wasn't serious like a lot of the other mothers and she did cool things like wearing sunglasses whether the sun was out or not. Just like my grandmother, my mother trusted me to go to the store to get things for her. One item I remembered getting for her was a box of ARGO starch. She would eat it all the time. Every now and then I would eat it, too. Never once did I ask her what it was for.

One thing she did not do very often was visit my grandmother. Moms could have walked from our apartment to Grandma's a million times a day. Instead, I was the one running back and forth from our house to Grandma's house if my mother wanted to tell my grandmother something. I liked to run and I liked to be out of the house. And I really liked doing things for my mother, so I didn't mind at all, even if it meant that I hardly ever saw my mother and grandmother in the same room at the same time.

In early June of 1968, I was 8 years old and finishing up the third grade. In a few weeks, the school year would be over. I was looking forward to playing with my friends all summer but first we had to get our trees.

At the end of every school year, the city of Scranton gave each student a plastic bag filled with a small plant. Our teachers encouraged us to plant them in our yards and water them every day. If you went to school in Scranton from kindergarten to high school, it was possible to have a dozen trees that you planted and helped to grow tall and strong.

Early in the morning of June 1, Moms came in late after a night of hanging out. My brother, Jeffrey, woke up to go to the bathroom and he saw her lying on the living room floor. He thought she had passed out so he tried to wake her. She wouldn't respond.

From then on, it was like a dream. The red and white lights from the ambulance lit up our apartment like an amusement park. People in uniforms rushed in and worked on my mom. They put Moms in the ambulance and drove off. We never ever saw her again.

As the sun came up in the morning, the house was full of people walking around and crying. Grandma was there and I remember that she was getting some of our clothes together.

"Why are all of these people in our house?" I asked my grandmother.

She turned to me and said, "You kids are staying over my house for a few days."

We were happy because Grandma's house was another home to us but this didn't feel like any other time we spent with her. Once there, she sat us down and told us that our mother was in heaven with God. How could that be? What was she talking about? Moms couldn't be in heaven. She was home just a few hours ago, getting ready to go out with her friends. Grandma told us that God always has a plan for our lives, even my mother's.

My grandmother's house was like a bus terminal. People were coming in and out all day. My family came in from Connecticut and other places. A few days later I remember we went to Bethel A.M.E. Church with Grandma. The church was filled with flowers and my mother was lying in a closed casket in the front of the church. Dawn, Jeffrey, Early, and I were the only ones in the whole church. Grandma sat us down in the front pew and she started praying. It still hadn't hit me that my mom was gone and I wondered what my grandmother felt about losing her youngest daughter.

Two weeks later we got out of school for the summer. On the last day of school, we got our plants. Grandma and Grandpa took us to the cemetery and we planted the trees on my mother's grave. After going to her gravesite, I cried for several days because that was when I realized I would never ever see my mom again.

The summer was not as fun as I had hoped. We were sad and really missed Moms. Although a lot had changed, some things stayed the same. My brothers and sister and I were back at my grandparents' house. We went to church every Sunday and still ate big Sunday dinners. I was still running errands for Grandma and even Mrs. Burgette and Mrs. Caddie if they needed anything but Grandma put a stop to our cleaning up the trash outside of Mo's Bar.

My grandparents had raised six children of their own. They had to decide what was best for us. Our father wasn't around and there was no way that Francis and Madeline Williams would let him get anywhere near us, even if my father wanted to. Yet, my grandparents had lived their lives and had raised their children. They just didn't have it in them to raise four more kids. My mother had a sister and two brothers who lived in Connecticut. The decision was made that we would be raised by them.

The summer of 1968 was about to end. One night, we played "hide and go seek." There were so many of us, both friends and family. Even Pam Moody was there. Pam was like a big sister to all of us. She was a few years older than Dawn and she was a lot of fun. She had three brothers and was used to playing with boys. When we played hide and go seek, we liked it when Pam was "it." She stood by one of the trees planted on Adams Avenue and called out the signals of the game. Once she left to find everyone who was hiding, I remember running to the tree as fast as I could. I was pretty good at hiding but I was the fastest runner out of all of us and never lost when we played hide and go seek.

By the time the game was over, it was getting dark, which meant we couldn't play anymore. It also was time to say goodbye to everyone.

We sat on grandma's front porch and Pam told us to behave up there in Connecticut. As hard as I tried to hold back my tears, I could not do it. My eyes were flooded with tears of sadness because I wasn't going to see my friends again after that night.

When it was time for bed, Grandma did the same thing she did when we slept at her house: she read us a bedtime story. We prayed before the story because most times we would all fall asleep before the story ended. Grandma wanted

25

us to talk to God before we went to bed and tonight was no different. She reminded us that God has a special plan for each of our lives and we had to promise her that we wouldn't forget that when we moved to our new home.

Leaving my grandparents in the morning was going to be harder than I thought. I didn't sleep well the night before. All I could think about was what it was going to be like living in Connecticut with my Aunt Thelma and her daughter, Lori. I had become so dependent on my grandparents and it would be a big adjustment not having them around.

Once the morning came, it was time to leave. My uncles had arrived from Connecticut the night before and were well rested for the day's journey to New England. Their plan was to leave early in the morning, so none of my friends or cousins was able to see us off.

I thought I cried the night before, but it was nothing compared to the tears that came that morning. Grandma talked to all of us in her bedroom about being respectful and behaving for our aunts and uncles. You could tell in her voice that she was sad to see us go. I hugged my grandmother like I was never going to see her again. Gramps shook our hands real hard and told us to behave like we had for Grandma. Tears streamed down my face as I got into the car and my journey began. I didn't know what God had planned for us but it couldn't be that good if he was taking me away from friends, my school, my church, and the best grandmother in the world.

Life has a funny way of changing its mind. One minute you're a kid playing games with your friends and the next you're wondering where you're going to live. When you're trying to focus on what comes next, it can be hard to focus on today and to let tomorrow take care of itself.

Yet all the small things we go through is what makes our lives unique. If we are blessed, life is an incredible and rewarding journey. But don't think about the long road ahead. Instead, think about taking one step, then another, then another. Before you know it, you'll start to see a pattern that leads to one simple fact:

**There is Always a Plan for
Your Life**

CHAPTER THREE

FAILING IS NOT THE END

The first thing I noticed when we arrived at our new home in New Britain, Connecticut was how different it was from my Scranton neighborhood. I didn't see any corner stores around and there weren't any houses with porches like there were on my grandmother's block. All I could see was street after street of two-story red brick buildings. This was where I was going to live. All of the houses were in rows of six and there was a softball field and a basketball court in the middle of the whole complex. My uncle told us that the place was called Corbin Heights. I liked the name because it sounded fancy. Later, I would learn that all housing projects had names that were nicer than the way the houses looked on the inside.

My Aunt Thelma—along with her daughter, Lori, who was about five years older than me—came to the car and greeted us. We unpacked the car but only took out what belonged to me, Early, and Jeffrey. That was when Uncle Erwin explained to us that Dawn was going to live with his family across town. We never knew that we were going to get split up. We had always been together and we didn't think that anything would change just because we had moved to Connecticut. We were crushed. Uncle Erwin could see that we weren't prepared to be separated but told us that Dawn would be fine. She would be sharing a room with her younger cousin, Lisa, who looked up to Dawn. He also told Dawn that living with his sons, Toby and Darryl, would be like living with her brothers. And he was happy that his wife, who we called Aunt Skee, would have another girl in the house to fuss over. But, to us, Dawn was the oldest and the leader of our family. We all started to cry but Uncle Erwin said that his house was not very far away and that we would see each other all the time.

Just like Grandma's house, my Aunt Thelma's house was very neat and there was plenty of food in the fridge and in the cabinets. That was where the similarities ended. It didn't take us long to realize that our living arrangements were going to be unlike anything we'd ever known. Aunt Thelma's house had two bedrooms: one for her and the other for Lori.

My brothers and I stayed in the finished basement. It wasn't too bad. In one area, there was a television, a couch and a few chairs on one side and a washer and dryer on the other. Our beds and dressers were in another area. My aunt had a husband, a man named Frankie Santiago. I thought it was strange that he didn't live with us. All the married people in Scranton lived in the same house. I guess a lot of things were going to be new in Connecticut.

Before we got settled in, Aunt Thelma went over her rules and expectations for us while living in her house. We had to stay mostly in the basement where we slept and watched TV and we could never, ever go in her bedroom. Although she looked and sounded like my mother and grandmother, it didn't take long before we realized that she was not as fun as our mother or as gentle as Grandma. I had gotten used to my grandmother as the most important person in my life. It was hard to imagine that I wouldn't see her every day and that I wouldn't get to watch her make sweet potato pies or fry catfish. But Grandma wanted me to respect Aunt Thelma, so I tried to stay out of trouble.

For the rest of that summer we made friends and played as boys typically seem to do. We saw Dawn as much as we could, just like my Uncle Erwin promised. Every other weekend, Aunt Thelma would take us over to Aunt Skee and Uncle

Erwin's house for Sunday dinner. They were the best aunt and uncle you could want; they lived in their own single family home on Whiting Street and not in the projects. Still, Dawn wanted to come and live with us. We missed having her around and wished that more things could have stayed the same.

In the fall, we all started in our new schools. We learned that Connecticut was like Scranton in some ways: lunch time and recess were the best parts of the school day. After school and on the weekends, we got to know our new neighborhood better. In our backyard there was a pharmacy called Millers. Next to that was a Kentucky Fried Chicken and a grocery store called the Mayflower. We never saw any variety stores or bars but that was okay with me. I didn't want to see anything that reminded me of what I missed about Scranton.

When the school year ended, we spent the summer in Scranton. I was so happy! I could play with my old friends and, best of all, I could spend as much time with my grandmother as I wanted. From that point on, we spent every summer in Scranton. I had two homes and two sets of friends and for me, this was my new normal.

In Scranton, all of my friends were black. Corbin Heights had all kinds of people: blacks, whites, and Puerto Ricans. Anyone could be your friend but the first friend I made in New Britain was Dana Vieira. He lived right across the driveway from us. He had an older brother and sister, Bert and Debbie. His mother, who I called Mrs. V., was a beautiful woman who treated me like I was one of her sons. Dana's father was the neighborhood father-figure and coach. Mr. Vieira, or Mr. V., got us involved with different sports. Dana was different from any friend that I had ever had. He had equipment for every sport and he had two pet alligators. Since we were in the same grade at Jefferson Elementary School, we hung out together. He would become my best friend.

We walked to school every morning but by the time 5th grade rolled around, we raced to school instead. Dana would win most of the time and our friend, Jeff Evans, usually came in second. If I couldn't come in first, I tried really hard to come in second. A few times, I almost beat Jeff. When 6th grade arrived, we started racing to school again and I was finally the fastest runner at Jefferson Elementary.

I loved being number one. I walked around the school with a swelled head and soon started fooling around in the classroom. After all, it was the last year in elementary school before we went to junior high school. I was in the same 6th grade class as my friend, Anthony Stevenson. We had a new teacher named Mrs. Buckout. Anthony and I drove her crazy every day but we were just having fun. Sometimes I felt sorry for her but most of the time I liked being the funniest kid in class and the fastest runner in my school.

In November, Mrs. Buckout handed us our report cards in class. When I opened it, I was in for the shock of my life. I had straight F's except for gym and art class. Dana and my other closest friends got good grades and during this time I wished I was more like Dana. How was I going to explain these grades to Aunt Thelma? She would kill me if she found out how bad I did in school. After thinking about it for a little while I went over to Anthony and asked him how he did. His report card was just as bad as mine. As we left the school at the end of the day, we knew that we were going to get in trouble at home. We decided to change some of the grades. We found pens with black and blue ink started turning our F's to B's and A's. Everything looked good and we walked home feeling much better about our report cards.

As soon as I got home, I gave the report card to Aunt Thelma. My brother, Early, got home before I did and had already showed her his report card. Once she took a look at mine she was so happy for me because she told me that I was a good student as long as I put my mind to work. She hugged me and I went outside to play. The next morning she signed it and gave it back to me so that I could give it to Mrs. Buckout. Anthony and I met on the way to school and stayed in the woods to change all of the grades back to the original grades.

There was a soft rain and we put the report cards in our pockets. When we returned the report cards, Mrs. Buckout asked us what happened to our report cards. They were damp from the rain and I was scared that she could tell that we tampered with them. She asked us a few more questions and then it was time to start our daily class work. The rest of the day went smoothly.

Everything changed the next day. It started with the race to school. One of the girls in my grade, Lynette, wanted to join our races. We never had any girls that wanted to race with us. I didn't mind Lynette racing with us because she couldn't beat me. Well, I was wrong. She beat me by a half step and all of the boys teased me because I let a girl win. Now, Lynette could say that she was the fastest runner in our school.

The rest of that day, I was miserable in school. When I got home, Aunt Thelma called me into her bedroom and asked me to close the door. She must have seen me walking home and could tell that I was upset about something. If she was my grandmother, she would have given me a hug and told me to run faster next time. But that's not what Aunt Thelma did. She asked me what happened to my report card that I had brought back to school. I explained to her that it got wet from the rain. She told me that Mrs. Buckout called and talked to her about my real grades. She was so angry with me that I was scared. My grandmother never made me feel afraid, even when she wasn't happy with me. Aunt Thelma sent me to my room as punishment and she kept yelling at me until I got to the basement.

I had just started to feel okay about living in Connecticut. Now, I wasn't so sure that this place was for me. I was failing 6th grade and a girl—a girl!—ran faster than me. Maybe I could call my grandmother and she would send some money so I could go back home and live with her. Or, maybe Rev. Burgette's boss would let him use their car so he could drive me back to my real home in Scranton.

Deep down I knew that I was stuck. There was no way I could go back to Scranton and there wasn't enough room for me at Uncle Erwin's house. I was going to have to live in Aunt Thelma's basement for a long time and I had to find a way to stay on her good side. When I returned to school the next day, I told Anthony that I wasn't going to be the class clown anymore and that I wanted to get better grades. As far as I was concerned, my days of fooling around in class were over.

◆ ◆ ◆ ◆ ◆ ◆ ◆ ◆ ◆ ◆

Being number one is the best feeling in the world. Everyone loves you because you are the smartest or funniest or fastest one around. People smile when you walk in the room and remember your name for all the right reasons. It feels like you are floating on air.

Maybe this is why failing hurts so much. One day we're making positive decisions about our lives and the next day we make one mistake that changes everything. The people who adored you now treat your poorly. You may not be able to change the way people treat you but you can recognize your mistakes and try to do better the next time. Just remember that each day you can start again because:

Failing is Not the End

CHAPTER FOUR

DREAM BIG, NOT SMALL

In just a few years, I went from being a little kid at Jefferson Elementary School to an older kid at Washington Junior High School to a teenager at Pulaski High School. Some things stayed the same: my siblings and I spent every summer in Scranton with our grandmother who was the most loving and stable adult in our lives. Dinky's family had moved away from Scranton but he came back like I did every summer and we went to the same camp. My cousin, Myron, still lived in Scranton and he joined us at camp, too. Two of my grandmother's closest friends, Mrs. Kearney and Mrs. Burgette, had passed away but so many people from my grandparents' neighborhood were still there living in the same houses, working for the same people, and going to the same churches. I was always glad to be in Scranton because back home in Connecticut, Aunt Thelma and I still didn't get along that well.

Even more things had changed in my life. Uncle Erwin died from lung cancer just three years after my mother died. About a year later, Dawn finally moved in with us; she shared a room with Lori. It was almost like old times because Dawn was there and that made everything easier to bear. Just when we were getting used to the old Dawn, we realized that she was growing up and becoming a young woman. In the winter of 1975, she gave birth to a son, Bryce. Dawn was a senior in high school but, when she got pregnant, she left to attend an alternative high school. She managed to earn her high school diploma on time. Aunt Thelma's house was pretty crowded by then, so after about a year, Dawn moved back to Scranton with Bryce. It was hard to get used to the changes in our family and I wished that things would stay the same for a while. It just didn't seem fair that I lost my mom and Uncle Erwin, then Dawn and Bryce.

Outside of Scranton, Pennsylvania and New Britain, Connecticut, the world around us was changing. In the fall of 1975, the Vietnam War had ended and everyone had a brother, uncle, son, or father who was on their way home. Some adults had jobs and others were looking for one. For the most part, we were still the kids who lived in Corbin

Heights who watched "Soul Train" on Saturday mornings and laughed at "Good Times" and "Sanford and Son" on TV. We rooted for the Dallas Cowboys and the Los Angeles Lakers and were sure that Muhammad Ali would beat Joe Frazier at the boxing match they were calling the "Thrilla in Manilla."

There were other changes I noticed. The black kids and the white kids at school didn't spend as much time together as we used to. We started to eat at different tables in the cafeteria and listened to different music. Dana Vieira's family moved out of Corbin Heights but he was still my best friend even though he went to New Britain High School. Our school, Pulaski High, was a small school with a population of about 600 students: there were only about 10 black students in the whole school, including me. I never really had any major problems in the school because my brother Jeff was really popular and was a captain of the football team. But after Papo died, I had a big decision to make.

Papo's real name was John Post and he was one of Jeff's best friends. Papo, who was black, dropped out of school after the 10th grade. I often saw Papo around the neighborhood with guys I had known since I moved to New Britain. Papo was a great basketball player but he also had a real tough side; no one messed with him and it kind of made sense that he formed a local gang out of the Malikowski Circle projects called the "Black Souls." Papo used to hang out with Frank Muir, a white guy with a bad temper. One night when they were hanging out, they got into a fight and Frank stabbed Papo to death.

The next day, the news was all over the school before the bell rang for first period. I worried about racial tension in the school but Papo's death changed the climate in the school. Some people defended Frank and said that Papo had it coming. All of the boys from the Circle were upset and at one point they wanted to retaliate. Race didn't make a difference when we were little kids at school. Now, race seemed to be at the center of everything.

The same day that we learned Papo died, I was walking in the hallway with some friends. When I arrived at my class, one of the girls asked me what happened to the back of my jacket. When I took it off to see what she was talking about, I saw a bunch of spit on the back of it. I immediately went to the front office and told them that I needed to go home and get a different jacket. While I was waiting in the office, a black student name Van Green ran into the office and a few white guys chased him there and were calling him a nigger outside the office window.

I went home that day and told Aunt Thelma that I was afraid that what happened to Papo might happen to me. I wasn't in a gang and didn't want to be, even though I heard stories about how protected I would be if I was in a gang. Still, there were only a few black kids at my school and that fact alone made me a target in the days after Papo died. I wanted to transfer to New Britain High School but I had to wait until after Thanksgiving. I was on the football team and New Britain High and Pulaski High always played a game on Thanksgiving morning. Dana was New Britain's best running back. I was a starting safety for Pulaski and my brother Jeff was a starter on both offense and defense. The Monday after Thanksgiving, my aunt drove me to Pulaski and withdrew me from the school. After getting all of the paper work we went directly to New Britain High School. I saw a lot of my friends from Washington Junior High School. I also had a lot of other friends who went to the other junior high schools in the city.

New Britain High School was much bigger than Pulaski. My new high school had a lot of diversity and I was more comfortable than I had ever been at Pulaski. Soon after my transfer, I had a chance to get a job. I wasn't getting any money at home so I needed every penny that I could get. At the same time, I really wanted to run on the indoor track team. The track coach was holding a meeting for those of us who were interested in joining the team. I went to the meeting and that was the first time I met Coach Irving Black. He wasn't tall but he was a broad shouldered man who wore thick black-rimmed glasses and had a headful of white hair. Coach Black had a very loud voice that made it sound like he didn't take any mess. Although I really wanted to run track, making some money was more important. Besides, Coach Black kind of scared me. I decided to work in an employment program for teenagers and I was placed at the high school as a student custodian. I worked for two hours a day cleaning the industrial arts rooms and enjoyed the job because I was getting paid every week.

During my first week on the job, I was cleaning the "wood shop" room and I heard this loud male voice call my name. I was so afraid that I hid behind a table in the room as the man entered the woodshop and kept calling out my name. It was Mr. Black, the track coach. I didn't even know him and I was scared of him. Well after he called my name a few times and I didn't answer he started walking out the door. I was trying to keep still but I knocked a piece of wood off one of the tables. He continued to walk out after he heard the noise.

The next day, one of my friends on the team told me that Coach Black made jokes about me hiding in the wood shop. I wasn't interested in being on a track team if the coach was going to make fun of me. I stayed away from Coach Black for the rest of the year and just kept on working. The money wasn't that much, but at least I was getting a check on Fridays. I was able to buy some things for myself. The rest of the school year went by fast because I had a job that I looked forward to each and every day.

Later that spring, my grandparents came up from Scranton because Jeff and our cousin, Darryl, graduated from high school. Darryl went into the Army that fall but Jeff chose to attend a prep school in Milford, Connecticut for a year to play football. Now only my younger brother, Early, and I were sharing the house with Aunt Thelma and Lori. There weren't as many people in the house but somehow it was like there wasn't enough space for me and Aunt Thelma together. My grandparents sensed the tension in the house but didn't say much about it. My grandparents, especially my grandmother, expected me to be grateful for having an aunt who was able to take care of so many kids at once. They were right and, if I was being honest, Aunt Thelma wasn't hard on me all the time. She got me transferred out of Pulaski High School and mostly acted like she was proud that I had a job. But I didn't feel grateful. I was caged and could not wait until I was old enough to leave her house.

When I was in my senior year at New Britain High School, I wanted to run indoor track more than ever. Coach Black had a loud voice but he wasn't mean. I was afraid that he might make fun of me if I made the track team but I was willing to put up with it. I had trained all summer and fall. Although a lot of my friends were on the football team, I decided not to play. I wanted to be ready for track. I had a chance to work again but I put everything on the side and concentrated on track.

Once the indoor season came around I had no idea what training was actually like until after my first high school track practice. I thought I would need a lot of energy to get through the intense workout Coach Black was famous for, so I ate a lot of food during lunch. But Coach Black's workouts and my eating plan was a bad combination; I started feeling sick and then I began vomiting. Everyone was laughing, which made everything worse for me. It was the last day that I would vomit at practice. I began to get in shape and things started getting better for me. Even my school work improved because Coach Black stressed to everyone on the team the importance of being a good student in the classroom and a good person out of the classroom.

The indoor season went pretty well, but the outdoor season was the best. During our conference track meet, which was called the C.D.C. championships, I placed first in the long jump and set a new meet record. I was so happy because transferring to the school the year before was paying off. Our team was great and we won the state outdoor track and field championships. The Monday after the state meet, Coach

Black met with all of the seniors individually to talk about our college plans. When he got to me, he asked me what college I applied to. I explained to him that my aunt and family didn't have any money and that I didn't fill out any applications. We were in his office and he told me to sit down while he made a phone call. As he was on the phone, I started to think about the first time that I met him and how I used to be afraid of him. But what I realized was just how much he supported his athletes.

While he was on the phone, he told whoever was on the other end that he had an athlete who wasn't very talented but that he would work hard. After a few other words, he placed the phone on the hook and said to me, "You are all set."

"All set for what?" I asked.

"You're headed to college," Coach said in his typical loud voice.

College? Didn't he just hear me say that college wasn't in my future? That my family didn't have any money for college and, even if they did, I hadn't filled out any applications? Coach Black said not to worry, that an application was coming to the school and I could fill it out when it arrived.

"Thanks, Coach," I said. Even if my family couldn't afford to send me away to college, at least I was going to Central Connecticut State University, which was right in New

Britain. That's when Coach Black started laughing and shaking his head.

"Central?!," he barked. "You're not going to Central, you're going to Kentucky. The school is a great track school and I sent a track athlete there two years ago and he is doing great. Don't worry about the money, once you fill out some financial aid papers you will get a lot of help."

I was shocked but I remembered what my grandmother taught me about being grateful when someone did something nice for me. I thanked Coach Black and went home to explain it to my aunt. She was happy as long as she wasn't paying for college but on the inside, I couldn't imagine how I was going to make it in Kentucky.

A few days later the paper work came in just like Coach Black said it would. That summer I got accepted to Kentucky State University. When it was time to go later that summer, I spoke with Coach Black. Coach was never an emotional man but I could tell that he cared about my welfare despite his tough exterior. Coach Black told me to look for a man named Dr. Exum as soon as I got to Kentucky State. Then he left me with words I'll never forget: "Go down there and make your family proud of you. Then come back and make a difference to some of the youth in the city." I had no idea what it meant to be a college student. And what could I do that would make a difference to anyone? If I went to this

48

college in Kentucky, I'd be leaving everyone I loved for a place I knew nothing about. But Coach Black was asking me to take a chance. I had to have faith that one decision at the right time would lead to bigger and better things.

Do you ever have those days where everyone you know is going in one direction but you want to go in the opposite direction? It's not that you're slow or afraid but there's a small voice deep inside you that is starting to guide your steps. That voice is the one that can help you to make positive decisions that will take your life to the next level.

Change is not easy but we have to have a plan that helps us to see ourselves in new ways. Sometimes that begins with making the smallest changes, like finding a new school or discovering a hobby or sport you really like. Maybe you have a Coach Black in your life to help you to begin to think about life outside of your comfort zone. Even if there isn't a teacher or mentor right now, a good place to start is by practicing this motto:

Dream Big, Not Small

CHAPTER FIVE

ADVANCE AND SURVIVE

In August of 1977, I boarded a plane heading to Pittsburgh, Pennsylvania with a connecting flight to Lexington, Kentucky. It was only the second time I flew in my life so I was a little nervous. The plane arrived in Lexington, during the middle of a steaming hot afternoon. After I picked up my suitcases, I boarded the van that would take me to the campus of Kentucky State University. We drove past horse parks and horse farms. Horses were everywhere. I honestly didn't know exactly where the school was and I was beginning to wonder if the school was in the countryside. The first day of class hadn't even started and I already had a lot of questions. I had heard that Kentucky was called the Blue Grass State, so where was all the blue grass? And why did the white folks have southern accents just like black folks?

After about thirty minutes the van arrived at the campus. There was activity everywhere, as people flowed in and out of the dorms. Students carried books and blankets, while their mothers chased after them saying things like, "Don't forget to…" and "Be careful…". The fathers were mostly silent, carrying the heavy boxes and suitcases. No one brought me to school. No one was there to unpack my things. It made me miss my mother and really made me miss having a father, even though I had been without parents for most of my life.

I made my way to my dorm, McCullin Hall. It was a three story brick building that I later found out was named after pilot Lt. James L. McCullin, who was one of the famous Tuskegee Airmen in WW II. As I entered the dorm, there were maybe two other people standing in the line besides me. The dorm director's name was Mr. Thaxton. He was a light-skinned black man and on the heavy side. He wanted to know my name. After I started to answer him, he began to laugh. Every word I said he laughed even more.

"Boy," Mr. Thaxton said to me. "Where are you from?"

"Connecticut," I said.

"Does everyone up there talk like you?" he asked. When I told Mr. Thaxton that I guessed so, he laughed again. He gave me my room key and told me there would be a freshman barbeque that evening. Then he asked if I wanted to room with someone from New York. That was the day that I met my roommate, Ronald Bateman, whose nickname was Mookie. I introduced myself as Darwin but told him he could call me Bubby.

I was amazed to see only black people on my new campus. By then, I had lived in Connecticut for most of my life and it was normal for me to be around people of all races. I didn't know until I got to Kentucky that my new school was a historically black college. It was like God painted the scene with only the richest shades of brown, from ebony to chestnut to vanilla. They called Washington, D.C. "Chocolate City," but on that first day of school you couldn't tell me that Chocolate City wasn't right here in the middle of Frankfort, Kentucky.

I was pretty sure that my brother, Jeff, was not at an all-black college. He spent a year at a prep school to make sure he was ready to play football in college. Then he left for Slippery Rock State College in Pennsylvania the same time I left for Kentucky. I wished Jeff and I were going to the same college and maybe we would have each other to lean on while we figured out what college was all about.

Freshmen orientation started early the next day. The workshops were in alphabetical order by last name, which meant that Mookie wasn't with me. When I arrived at my first workshop I thought I was in the wrong place. Every student in the room was dressed in suits and dresses, like they were going to church instead of freshmen orientation. Maybe I missed something in the schedule that said we had to dress up. I didn't own a single suit. But that didn't matter to the folks from big cities like Chicago and Detroit: the men wore alligator shoes and three piece suits and the women wore really fancy dresses! I learned later that fashion was important to the students who came from cities or from upper middle class families. But getting dressed up to go to class was not a luxury that I could afford.

If fashion was important, so was the way you spoke. During that first workshop, everyone introduced themselves. I was the only one who didn't have a Southern accent. They all wanted to know what my name was and where I was from. According to my new classmates, I talked proper. I would never call the way I talked "proper," but I guess it was. My grandmother stressed the importance of speaking English well. She was really my first teacher and corrected me the minute she heard me mumbling or talking slang. I tried to sound like I was intelligent and spoke as clearly as I could. When I was around my friends, I added a little slang here and there. Other than that, I spoke the only way I was taught. This was one of the first things I learned in college.

There was one person I met who was from Chicago and who became an instant friend: Greg Harris. You could tell he was from the city by the way he dressed and walked. He had a boldness about him but he got along with everyone. Greg never made fun of the way I talked and it didn't bother him that I did not own a suit. Chicago wasn't too far from Frankfort, Kentucky and soon I was riding with him to the Windy City for several weekends during the school year.

There was a two hour break between workshops. Coach Black wanted me to meet Dr. Exum as soon as I could, so I walked over to Bell Gymnasium. There were people playing volleyball and basketball. I found Dr. Exum's office and knocked on the door. A man with a really soft voice told me to come in. As I entered the room, I saw this older man with a bald head and a thin build.

"Are you Dr. Exum?" I asked nervously.

"Yes," he answered. "And who might you be?" I told him my name and that my high school track coach told me to find him once I got to Kentucky.

Dr. Exum smiled and asked me to take a seat. If you were a student at KSU, if you worked at KSU, or if you lived nearby, you knew all about Dr. William Exum. Dr. Exum had been the ultimate student athlete of his time. He was a football and track star at University of Wisconsin in the 1920s and 30s and earned three college degrees, including his doctorate. It wasn't easy for Dr. Exum. At one point, his professors said his grades weren't very good, which made him ineligible to play any sports for his school. In the midst of an all-white student body, he was the first black player on the football team and excelled on the track team; it wasn't hard to guess what role racism might have played. By the time we met, Dr. Exum had been the head of the Physical Education department and the KSU athletic director for almost 30 years. Dr. Exum was probably the best person to ever to coach track at KSU. He was our father, our grandfather, our very own champion.

We talked for about an hour, mostly about his friendship with Coach Black and what my plans were for college. I told Dr. Exum that I hadn't really thought about a major. He asked if I ever thought about being a teacher. I didn't waste any time telling him that I didn't want to be a teacher.

Dr. Exum paused and asked, "How many black male teachers did you have growing up?"

I could think of only two: Mr. Harris, who taught at my elementary school and Mr. Springer, who was at my high school.

Dr. Exum didn't tell me what to major in but he said this: *Go back home and make an impact on some of the youth in your city.* That conversation stayed with me for the rest of the week. From that day on, Dr. Exum would call me Mr. Shaw.

Orientation week was long. I never realized there was so much to learn. My classes were in different buildings and I only had a few minutes to get from one building to the next. I had to do my laundry, figure out when to eat, and get used to living with people I had only known for a few days.

One of the biggest shocks was when I learned about an important part of the social life at KSU: fraternities and sororities. I had no idea about fraternities and sororities until I got to college. One of the tours during orientation took us to the University bookstore. Our school colors were green and gold, so I wasn't surprised to see shirts, jackets, and school supplies in those colors. But then I saw the same items in red and black, pink and green, gold and black, crimson and cream, red and white, purple and gold, and more. Those colors were all over campus, even painted on rocks.

I would see groups of people hanging out together wearing those colors. At the end of the freshman orientation week, they were having something called a step show on the lawn in front of the library. There were hundreds of students watching the different groups marching, singing, and dancing. I had entered the world of black Greek life. Actually, I was watching from the outside. Becoming a member of a fraternity would take a lot more than asking. All I was told was that I could go to an interest meeting if I wanted to learn more.

Besides hanging out with only the people who wore the same color clothes and participating in step shows, I had no idea what fraternities and sororities did. I had plenty of time to figure that out. I was only interested in the day I could wear my school's gold and green as a member of the track team.

That fall, my days were filled with classes and track practice. Every week was the same: practice at 5:30am, breakfast around 7:30, classes starting at 8 and back to track practice at 4:00pm. Coach Black may have paved the way for me to be admitted to college but as far as the track team went, I was a walk on and had to earn a spot on the team. There was only one other jumper. His name was Dale Long and he was a sophomore from Springfield, MA. We trained almost every day together and we called each other homeboys because we lived so close to each other back home.

The only other freshman on the team was Doug. He told people that he was from the Bronx, not that he had to tell people that he wasn't from the South. All the New Yorkers, including Mookie, bonded together right away. I guess they included me because I was from the north.

The track and field coach was Ken Gibson. Doug and Coach Gibson were close because Coach was also from New York. I never really had a good bond with Coach because it seemed like he was only interested in the athletes that he recruited. Coach Gip, as the other athletes called him, had his favorites. Three of them were All-Americans: Greg Anderson from Detroit, Hamil Grimes from Barbados and Craig Maree, who came from a small town outside of Detroit. Greg and Hamil were very quiet and laid back but Craig was a different story. He liked to be the center of attention by being loud, cracking jokes, and making fun of people on the team. I think he was like that because he was a muscular guy and no one would try him because of his size and strength. If Craig really got going, Greg had to tell him to cool off and stop talking about people. Craig respected Greg a lot and would stop without hesitation. They also belonged to the same fraternity, Kappa Alpha Psi. I learned that being in a fraternity made them as close as brothers.

By January, it was time for our first meet at Indiana University in Bloomington, Indiana. I made the traveling team and I was very excited. Doug and Dale also were on the list. We took a van to the meet and there must have been about 15 of us. Coach Gip was the driver. For most of the trip everyone was sleeping, except Craig. He was in rare form. But as we got closer and closer to our destination, the mood in the van turned serious. There was no more joking or teasing one another, as the veteran runners started to concentrate and focus.

When the announcement came for all long jumpers to report, I went over with Dale. The head official put two flags on the outside of the sand pit and explained that if we did't jump past that mark, our jump would not be measured. If your jump wasn't measured, it would not count. It would be like not jumping at all. The mark was 22 feet. I had only jumped that distance once in my life and in practice we never jumped for distance. Dale wished me good luck and the competition started. None of my jumps came close to 22 feet; Dale didn't do any better. We didn't know how far we jumped, we just knew it wasn't 22 feet. Coach Gip never bothered to come to the long jump area to see how we were doing but I didn't need him to make me feel bad.

I had let myself down. Once the long jump was over I watched the 400 meters. Greg and Hamil took 1st and 2nd places and then they took first place in the 4x400 meter relay that they ran with Craig. We stopped at a restaurant before the long ride back to campus. Craig bragged about what he did on the relay team and started getting on most of the newcomers for not doing anything but riding to the meet for nothing and eating a free meal. It didn't help that I wasn't in a fraternity and that I was still trying to earn my spot; Craig wasn't going to make it easy for me and there wasn't a lot I could do to stop him.

◆ ◆ ◆ ◆ ◆ ◆ ◆ ◆ ◆ ◆ ◆

Sometimes life seems very simple: you do one thing well and move on to the next. You are proud of yourself for staying focused on your goals. You march into every situation determined to succeed. But what happens when taking those steps gets more difficult? Or when the people around you are waiting for you to fail?

Life would be amazing if it came without obstacles. But if everything came easy, we wouldn't have the chance to learn if the goals we've set are really important to us. Meet each challenge as it comes, no matter how impossible things look at the time. If you do this, then you will discover that meeting small goals—one step at a time—helps you to:

Advance and Survive

CHAPTER SIX

EVERY DECISION MATTERS

The next track meet was at the University of Illinois in Champaign, Illinois. This time, Dale and I prepared for the measurements at the long jump as if the rules would be the same as Indiana University. We had trained really hard since the last meet. All we could think of was 22 feet. It was like nothing else mattered. Not our classes or parties or our friends. If this was New Britain High School, Coach Black would be pushing me to be my best. But this wasn't Connecticut and Coach Black wasn't there. I was still trying to make the team and could not count on Coach Gibson to be supportive. I was invisible to him.

Dale and I brought our own tape measure so we could keep track of how far we jumped. During the competition, Dale and I both put marks on the side of the pit. After the competition ended, we took out our tape measure and measured where we jumped. My best jump was 20′ 8″. While we were measuring, good ole teammate Craig saw us. I told myself that I was wasting my time doing track in college because I jumped better when I was in high school. Illinois turned out to be just like our first meet in Indiana; our jumps weren't long enough to reach the flags. Dale and I were heartbroken but at least we knew how far we had jumped, even if the track officials said our jumps didn't count.

I asked myself what I was doing there. I was going to college 800 miles away from home, people still teased me for talking proper, and it was impossible to make the KSU track team. Every day, I could hear Coach Black's words: "Go down there and make your family proud of you." Well, going to college wasn't my idea. I wasn't exactly the best student in my high school and I still didn't know what I wanted to study in college. If I was like my brother Jeff, I would have been a student athlete the first time I set foot on campus. Jeff didn't have to worry about making the track team and making our family proud. That, unfortunately, was my job.

On the long ride home, Craig couldn't stop talking about me and Dale. Craig kept talking about the tape measure that we brought on the trip. He had the whole van laughing for hours. I really wished that he would lay off and I started talking about how he was only a relay runner and not a good individual runner and that he was taking the glory for being a part of a relay team. The words coming out of my mouth didn't feel like me. I was the peaceful but friendly guy, the one you could count on to be funny but not mean. But I was Craig's punching bag and I had had enough. I told him that if it weren't for the relay, he would be coming home after every meet without any medals.

That made Craig mad. He started teasing so bad that I had tears in my eyes. Craig and some of the guys thought I was just some kid from Connecticut who had no chance of being a track star. I was glad that it was dark on the van and that there was music playing on the radio. That way, no one could see or hear how upset I was that night. I guess it didn't matter in the end because that was my last trip of the season.

Besides classes and track and field—and the occasional party—there wasn't a lot to do at Kentucky State. It was located in Frankfort, which is the capital of Kentucky. For a capital, it was a small city with a winding river that you could see almost everywhere you went. Frankfort also had historic houses that visitors toured all the time. There were a lot of parks but not the kind I was used to with at least one basketball court. The parks in Frankfort had mowed lawns, flower beds, and paved walkways. If you liked horseback riding and picnics in the park, you were in the right city.

Frankfort was not the type of city that would interest 18 year-old college students. We liked the city of Lexington. It was a 30 minute drive from our campus but at least it was more exciting than horses and house tours.

The school year was about to end and we were bored. Our friend, Fox, was the only one with a car. One Saturday, he took me, Doug, and Mookie to Lexington to go shopping. We had the windows down while we were riding and the music was blasting to the sounds of Cameo. Just before we got to the mall, we decided to stop at a sporting goods store. The new Dr. J. Converse All-Stars were on the shelf. They were white leather high tops with a star on the side. I really liked them but I didn't have enough money to get a pair, so I decided to continue looking at the hats. Mookie asked all three of us if we wanted a pair of sneakers. "It's my treat," he said. For a second, I thought 'how could it be his treat?' Mookie was like the rest of us: a college student with no money. But Mookie had been my friend since the first day of college. He always had my back. I was so excited that I didn't even have to try mine on. I told the store clerk that I wanted a size 10 ½ in the white and sky blue North Carolina colors.

When the store clerk brought the sneakers out, Doug and I noticed that Mookie and Fox had already left the store. They must have forgotten that we were in the store. When Doug and I got up to the front of the store, we grabbed our sneakers and walked out the door because Mookie had already paid for them. We caught up with Mookie and Fox as they were getting into the car. Fox turned on the car really quick and took off. We asked why they didn't tell us that they were leaving. Mookie said the store owner ran the credit card and found out that it wasn't his. Mookie had been charging stuff for a few days but that was the first time that they asked him for any identification. We had four pairs of sneakers in the car that no one paid for. Mookie knew we were in trouble, which is why they left. If Fox and Mookie had stopped to get our attention, there was no way the store owner would have let Mookie go.

In the meantime, the store owner had gotten into his car and was following us. Fox thought that he would be in the most trouble because he was driving what was now the getaway car. We threw our sneakers out of the window but that didn't stop the store owner from following us. After a few minutes there was a police car chasing us and we all got real scared. We were on a little bridge when Fox finally pulled over. Out of nowhere about five police cars showed up with sirens blaring. We were separated and handcuffed. They took us to separate cars and questioned us. I had never been handcuffed before. After sitting in the police car by myself for about 30 minutes, an officer started walking toward the police car that I was in. I thought he was getting ready to let me go.

Well, it didn't matter what I was thinking, because once the police officer got to the car he started it up and he drove off. I asked him where we were going and he told me that I was going to jail for a long time but that my friends were let go. I couldn't believe that my friends had blamed me for using that stolen credit card. When I got to the police station, they removed the handcuffs and put me in a cell for a few hours. Then they took me out and brought me to get fingerprinted and they took a photo of me holding up a card with numbers on it. That is when I started to get the feeling that I might be in jail for a while. Later, I was brought to a bigger room. There must have been over 100 prisoners in there. I sat in a corner and started praying. I lost track of time. I started walking around and I noticed a group of about 20 guys in one section of the room. As I got closer to the group I saw Fox, then I saw Mookie and Doug. If they were in jail, it meant that they didn't blame me for using that credit card.

But I wasn't feeling that much better. There wasn't much to talk about and some of the other guys in the cell asked us where we were from and what we did to get arrested. Some of the guys were telling us that we might get at least five years of prison because we were from the east coast. Even if we didn't do anything, we were guilty by association. We had to stay in jail until Monday morning because there was no court on the weekends. I prayed the entire time. I prayed like my grandmother taught me. I prayed like God was right in the room listening to me. I told God that if he got me out of jail, I would lead a good, clean life. I promised God that I wouldn't drink or use profanity and that, from now on, I would be very careful about choosing my friends. Those were the two longest days of my life.

Finally, Monday morning came and I was the first one from my group called in by the judge. I pleaded not guilty. The store owner was there and explained to the judge that I wasn't the one who signed the credit card. The judge ordered that I had to pay a restitution fine of $178.00 and that I couldn't leave the state of Kentucky until it was paid. I was released shortly after that.

Later that Monday, Fox and I went back to school. Most of our friends already heard what happen. Doug was also back on campus but he only lasted until the end of our freshman year. Mookie left Kentucky as soon as he was released from jail. That Tuesday I went to track practice. My teammates were acting strange around me but I didn't care. I just wanted to forget about the weekend and get back to normal. That wasn't going to happen. Coach Gibson told me that I was dismissed from the team due to my arrest.

I thought I had let myself down that first track meet. That was nothing compared to being arrested and getting kicked off the track team. I had failed myself and everyone who ever cared about me. But, in a way, it wasn't all bad. I was not kicked out of school and I didn't have to go to prison. As I packed my belongings to go home for the summer, I had a tiny bit of faith that told me that I would get through all of this. I didn't know how, I just knew that I would.

◆ ◆ ◆ ◆ ◆ ◆ ◆ ◆ ◆ ◆ ◆

You are not perfect. No one has to tell you this. You've learned how to read people and situations so you don't walk into anything that's dangerous or harmful.

But sometimes, you turn down the volume on your inner voice. Your better judgment says to go left and you go right. And you make the worst decision of your life. Trust the voice that tells you the best thing to do. Every day, you have to make decisions that will have lasting consequences. Get in the habit of trusting your inner voice because:

Every Decision Matters

CHAPTER SEVEN

CHOOSE YOUR ROLE MODELS WISELY

The summer after my first year in college started out like most of my summers. I was back in Scranton spending time with my grandparents for a few weeks. My grandmother was as close as ever to Mrs. Haynes and Mrs. Caddy still had me running errands for her. As long as people liked candy, Jack's Sweet Shop wasn't in danger of going out of business. Mo's Bar was still the place to be on a Friday night. I had heard my father was around but I wasn't going to waste my time looking for him. I did make time to visit my mother's best friend, Anita Jackson. She was the closest I could get to my mother. Sometimes I visited Miss Jackson only because I needed to feel like my mother was still alive. When I really missed Moms, I went to the cemetery. The trees we planted just after she died were growing tall and strong. I wished that I was in a park talking to Moms about college instead of visiting her lonely grave.

The summer of 1978 was full of awkward moments. I had been to college and had planned on telling my grandparents about how proud I was to be going to a historically black college and how proud it made me to see so many black people going to school so that they could make the world a better place. I wanted to tell my grandparents about my classes and the professors who acted strict but only wanted the best for us. And I wanted to tell my grandparents what it was like to be on a college track team. But I didn't feel I had a right to tell those positive stories. Instead, I had to face my grandparents, who had learned about my arrest from Aunt Thelma.

My grandfather didn't say much. He was the quiet one and wasn't the disciplinarian. When I was a kid, my grandfather's job as a porter for the railroad kept him away as much as a month at a time. He wasn't really around to see us grow up and probably felt that he didn't have a right to say too much about what his grandkids did or did not do. On the other hand, my grandmother let me know that she was very disappointed with me. I couldn't blame her. My grandparents had done so much for me and my siblings after our mother died. My grandparents were wise enough to know that it wasn't always easy to live by the morals and values they taught me but they expected me to try. My grandmother let me know that I went to Kentucky State to further my education and that I should never let anything distract me from doing just that. As hard as that was to hear from her, my grandmother was ultimately a caring, Christian woman who reminded me that everyone makes mistakes. She prayed that I had learned from my mistake and she encouraged me to move on with my life. It was good advice but hard to put into practice. She would never know that I was no longer on the track team and I didn't have it in me to break her heart twice.

After visiting with my grandparents, I spent the rest of the summer at home in New Britain. My cousin, Lori, was now the mother of an infant son, who she named Jack; they continued to live in the house where we grew up. My younger brother, Early, had gone back to Scranton. Aunt Thelma got married but the marriage didn't last long and she moved to an apartment on Pierremont Avenue in New Britain. When I came home for break, my aunt told me that I could live with her. I never believed that she let me live with her because I was her favorite nephew. As long as she let me live with her while I was in college, she got money from the state. It wasn't an ideal situation but I needed someplace to call home during the summer. That apartment had to be good enough.

Outside of my family situation, I had to have something that kept me busy and happy. I was lucky enough that summer to run for a club called the New Britain Striders Track and Field Club. All of the runners were connected to New Britain High School, either as former track runners or as students who were still in school. It was a time for us to stay connected with each other and work out. We practiced about four times a week and performed in track meets in the state on weekends. None of them had heard that I got kicked off of the team at KSU.

Running occupied my time but I also needed money. I found a job as a playground aide at the Corbin Heights housing project. I was responsible for about 25 kids every day. Sometimes it was tough to keep them involved in team sports, individual sports, arts and crafts, and feed them breakfast and lunch. We would take them to Osgood Park and go swimming most afternoons when it was too hot to do anything else. No one showed me how to teach kids; the only thing I had to go on was that I had known most of those kids all of their lives and had grown up with their brothers and sisters. What I did know was that there was an important lesson that stayed with me as a kid: be kind to others. Every day, I treated the kids with kindness even when there were times I did not want to. Within a few weeks, I found a rhythm to my days and discovered that the kids really listened to and respected what I had to say.

That fall, I returned to Kentucky State for my sophomore year. This time, I was just a college student and not a student athlete. Before the end of my freshman year, I had decided to major in physical education and minor in health education. Dr. Exum was my academic advisor and he helped me to see that my love of sports could lead to a pretty good life as a teacher. It was natural for me to study what I loved but I often found it hard to be motivated about my classes. But I went to classes anyway and spent time with my friends. Spring semester came and it was the same. Nothing exciting happened and I guess I should have been grateful for that. But I missed being on the track team more than I ever thought I would.

The summer of 1979 helped me to forget about school. I had a pretty good summer back home with my friends. If I didn't have anything to celebrate in terms of my college track career, I was glad to have friends who were doing really well. Two of my former high school teammates, Rich Edwards and David "Pom Pom" Mobley, were ranked on the top twenty lists in their track events. David ran track for Western Kentucky University, while Rich ran track for University of Houston. We spent a lot of time during the summer hanging out and talking about winning the state championship in 1977. Although I was happy for them, I wished that one day I would get a chance to run again at KSU.

In early fall 1979, I was heading back to Kentucky State for my junior year. My expectations for school weren't really low but they weren't very high. My goal was to pass my classes, which was getting harder to do. I was thinking about being a teacher but still wasn't sure that was what I wanted to do as a career. A year had passed and I was missing track. Without track, I didn't know if there was any point in going to college other than to make my grandmother proud.

On the day that I was flying back to Lexington, I had a layover in Washington D.C. for about an hour. While I was waiting at my gate and reading a magazine, this huge person about 7 feet tall walked into the area where I was sitting. He was a young, fair-skinned black man about my age and carried a pool case with the name "BOWIE" on it. Once I saw that name, I said to myself, *That's Sam Bowie, the number one high school basketball player in the country!* He sat right across from me, his long legs taking up most of the space in front of him. He looked directly at my track bag, which had "Kentucky State University Track & Field" written on it.

"Do you go to that school?" he asked. I told him yes and he started to tell me his name.

"I know who you are," I said, trying not to act too excited. "You're Sam Bowie, the number one high school player in the country. My name is Darwin Shaw." Then I said, "But my friends call me Bubby."

We talked about going to the University of Kentucky and playing basketball. I told him that the players at University of Kentucky were the biggest celebrities in the state. Sam was not the type to brag but he told me that he was a member of the number one recruiting class in the country. I laughed and told him that I knew all about that because I had read an article about him in Sports Illustrated.

At the time, Sam Bowie was one of the biggest names in high school and college basketball. Parade magazine, Scholastic magazine, and McDonald's all named him to their All-American teams. At over 7 feet tall, big was an understatement. Sam was the National Player of the Year and every school wanted him to play for them. In the end, he chose University of Kentucky and played so well for the Wildcats that at the end of his freshman year he was chosen for the 1980 Olympic men's basketball team. He wouldn't get a chance to play in those Olympics because that was the year that the United States boycotted the games, which were played in Russia. Even if Sam didn't get to compete in the Olympics, he and the other athletes who missed the games that year still got gold medals courtesy of the United States

Congress. And when it came time for the 1984 NBA draft, the Portland Trailblazers chose Sam for their second overall pick, right after Hakeem Olajuwon was drafted by the Houston Rockets but before Michael Jordan was drafted third by the Chicago Bulls. But that day at the airport, we were just two students on our way to college.

Finally it was time for us to board the plane and he asked if it was okay to sit together when we got on the plane. So we flew from Washington, D.C. to Lexington and had a great conversation for the 45 minute flight. Before we got off the plane at the Lexington airport, Sam said that one of the coaches was picking him up but he wanted to get my address and phone number when we got inside the terminal. I told him that once he got inside, I wouldn't be able to get to him because all of the media from across the state would probably be inside the terminal. As soon as we got inside, the media was there just like I said it would be. The coach easily found Sam and hustled him out of the terminal before I could give him my number. All Sam could do was wave at me.

When I got to my campus it was good seeing most of my friends again. I let them know that I flew back with Sam Bowie. I was sorry that Sam and I couldn't exchange contact information but I had a plan I was sure would work. After I registered for my classes the next day, I went looking for my friend, Todd. He had a car and I told him that we needed to take a ride to UK, which is what we called the University of Kentucky. He was excited to meet Sam himself, so we took the drive south to Lexington.

The University of Kentucky campus was huge. We had to find a place called the Wildcat Lodge. The UK mascot was a wildcat, so it wasn't unusual to see the wildcat name everywhere on that campus. But the Wildcat Lodge was different. It was a separate dormitory for the UK men's basketball players. The dorm housed fewer than 40 athletes but it took up an entire block. The building stood out from the other buildings on campus. The Wildcat Lodge was supposed to look like an old hunting lodge but it was made of gray cement not wood. Small rectangular and round windows made it hard to see inside the building. A long walkway lead to double doors, where a guard monitored who came in and who came out.

After we found Wildcat Lodge and parked the car, we started walking to the front entrance. As we got closer, this security guard came over and told us that we couldn't get into the dorm and that it was for players only. I told him that I was a friend of Sam Bowie's and he said that Sam wasn't in there and that he saw him leave a while ago. Todd and I decided that we would wait for a little while to see if he showed up. The guard told us that we couldn't wait in the parking lot closest to the Lodge but if we wanted to we could wait for Sam across the street.

Well, we waited and waited. After two hours, we saw Sam walking toward the Lodge all by himself. The security guard pointed him out and Todd and I got out the car and started walking toward Sam. As I approached Sam, he turned to me and said "What's up, Bubby?" I was shocked that he remembered my name. After we exchanged handshakes, I introduced Sam to Todd and then Sam took us inside the dorm we had heard so much about. We hung out for about an hour with Sam and that was the beginning of our relationship.

I made several trips to UK during that first semester and Sam and I got to be very close friends. I went to several exhibition and then regular season games and attended many of the post-game receptions with Sam. Even if he wanted to, there was no way that Sam could come to my campus. His life as a student athlete was run like a tight ship: practice, classes, games, team meetings. When I was on the track team, we had to keep a schedule, too, but nothing as closely monitored as Sam's. He was a college student but in reality, being a student athlete was as serious to him as having a job.

When I watched Sam play, he was focused on what he had to do. Basketball was definitely more of a team sport than track but Sam wasn't just a member of the team. He had a desire to be the best athlete he could be. Of course he had the UK coaches, trainers, and assistants to help him to stay focused. Even if Sam didn't have all those people around to help him, I think he would have done everything he could to guard against anything that might have threatened his chance to play. It's a step I did not make in my own life. I lived with the consequences of my decisions every day I wasn't a college athlete.

Meeting Sam was one of the bright spots in my life at the time. But there was much better news for me when I returned to my campus after Todd and I found Sam at UK. I was heading to the student center and I saw Wayne, one of my former track teammates. He asked me if I was going to run track now that Coach Gibson was gone. I said, "What do you mean he's gone?" Coach Gibson had left KSU to coach track at another university and the new track coach was a football assistant coach named Clark Frost. Wayne told me that the team meeting was scheduled for the next week and I should show up. I had been praying to God for another chance since I got dismissed from the team and finally, maybe, my dreams were being heard and answered.

After speaking with Wayne, there was one person I needed to see: Dr. Exum. He was in his office as I expected. He heard about Coach Frost's arrival and was not at all surprised that I wanted to try out for the track team again.

However, there were two issues that had the potential to destroy my dream before it got a chance to come to life. One challenge was that I needed someone who saw my potential and who would help train me during the outdoor track season. But the greatest challenge was that my grades had slipped and I wouldn't be eligible to run until outdoor season anyway. Dr. Exum agreed to help me to train but told me to get my academics in order and the track situation would take care of itself.

A week later, I attended the meeting and met Coach Frost. I explained to him that I used to run track for KSU and that I was let go by Coach Gibson. I didn't even have to explain the situation to him about the sneakers or my arrest. All Coach Frost said was that this was a new year and that if I wanted to join the team that I was welcome with open arms. I left there and thought that life for me had started all over again. Except for my good friend, Dale, I didn't know most of the athletes on the team. I didn't let that bother me. I had a long time to live with the consequences of my decision during my freshman year. And while I missed running track, I got to know Sam, a person with the kind of drive, ambition, and humility that I really admired. Now, I had been given a second chance and I was determined to become the type of person that would make Dr. Exum and my grandmother proud. But more than that, I wanted to look in the mirror and finally respect the man staring back at me.

It's hard to imagine life without your friends. They're probably the people you work with or maybe you go to the same school. You spend a lot of time together and, for the most part, you wouldn't have it any other way. Yet, deep down, you know something is missing. Your friends are decent people but they don't inspire you to be a better person.

A good friend has qualities you admire and sometimes that good friend becomes a role model. Find people who are smarter than you, who are willing to tell you when you're doing something great and when you're not. It's great to have a friend whose main goal is to have a good time. But if you are going to become a better person, you need to:

Choose Your
Role Models Wisely

CHAPTER EIGHT

OPPORTUNITY IS EARNED, NOT GIVEN

O nce the spring of 1980 came, I was in tip top shape. The regular practice time was from 4:00pm to 5:30pm. Coach Frost allowed me to come to practice late because my classes didn't end until 4:30pm. So by the time I got to the track, everyone was just about finished with their workouts. That was fine with me because I didn't know many of my teammates and it was fine with Coach Frost since I wasn't eligible yet to run indoor meets.

While my athletic life was slowly getting back to normal, I couldn't say the same thing about my classes.

After I got kicked off the team after my freshman year, school wasn't that important to me. My grades were awful throughout sophomore year and through the beginning of my junior year. I took Introduction to Literature but there was too much reading and writing, so I took the easy way out by dropping the class. I was registered to take a track class because it was required for all P.E. majors but I ended up withdrawing from that class and any other class that reminded me that I was not on the track team. I also dropped a psychology course, couldn't pass Anatomy and Physiology, no matter how hard I tried, and I barely passed Physical Science.

For someone majoring in physical education and minoring in health education, I was a long way from being a model student. Dr. Exum took every chance to remind me that it was my future and if I wanted to mess it up, then I was doing a great job at it. He was one of the few people who understood how much trouble I was in academically. I honestly felt that Dr. Exum was more disappointed in me than I was in myself. My friends would never know how terrible I was doing in school. Not even my Aunt Thelma knew because once the grades got mailed home I would get them from the mailbox. She would just take my word that I was doing okay. Later, I would take those classes again and pass them but not before I learned some tough lessons about getting second chances.

Dr. Exum's reputation was unparalleled on campus and in the world of track and field. For a small number of us, Dr. Exum was also our professor who taught classes like Tests & Measurements and Kinesiology. Of course, he was my professor for both of those classes.

Science was not my thing. If I had known that I had to take a lot of science classes for my major, I probably would have chosen something else to study. But it was too late to select another major.

Dr. Exum called on me during every class. Whenever I walked with him to his office after class, he would tell me that I better study because, if I didn't, he would embarrass me in front of the class. One day he called on me to answer a simple question but I didn't answer it correctly. Dr. Exum was not happy. In front of the entire class, he said that whatever kind of studying I was doing, I had better change it.

Another time, we were in Kinesiology class and Dr. Exum was lecturing about the bones in the body. He called me in front of the class and made me pull off my shirt. He said your body is nothing but bones and everyone can see yours. I was so mad and embarrassed that I almost didn't show up for his class the next time but he would attack me more if I was absent from his class even once. From then on, I never missed Kinesiology or Tests & Measurements. I was never going to be a scientific genius but if I wanted to be a teacher I had to pass those classes. I earned a C in both of those classes, which, at the time, was like an A to me. I was learning to be more positive about my classes and hoped that would translate to my not so great track career.

I went to track practice every day but I wasn't getting much better. By this time, Dr. Exum was a trusted confidante who I had started to call "Doc." I told Doc that Coach Frost wasn't really helping me with my long jumping. One day, I asked Doc if he had any free time to stop at the track and help me with my jumping technique. Doc was a manager on the U.S. Olympic men's track and field team in 1972 and in 1976. If anyone had a clue about what they were talking about it when it came to track, that person would be Doc. He agreed to meet me at the track at least twice a week. After I worked out with him on those days, he often shared stories about his days at University of Wisconsin. He talked about what he had to face as a young black man on a predominantly white campus at a time when black men were open targets for racial hatred. He talked about how he could never separate his love for sports from his love for learning. Every sports failure, like when he injured his ankle and almost didn't play football for the University of Wisconsin Badgers in 1934, taught him that he had to fight harder to get back in shape. As a professor and a coach, he was tough but on those spring days, Doc was becoming my mentor.

On the days that I didn't work out with Doc, I ran the hills of Cold Harbor Drive. It was a street that rose above the hills near the main campus of KSU. When I ran there, it was so quiet that the only sound I heard was when my feet hit the pavement. Thick woods lined either side of the street. On one side, the remains of an old stone wall was covered with bushes and vines.

Most of the time I would run to the president's house before making my way back to the main campus. The president's house was a few hundred feet from the street. It may have just been a very large house but it looked like a mansion with light colored bricks, white columns and a massive front double door. The long driveway was beside the biggest front lawn I had ever seen. I loved to run by there because the patterns from the lawnmower made the grass look like a carpet that had just been vacuumed.

Doc also lived on Cold Harbor Drive, right next to the track. His part of the street had large front yards and brick ranch style homes with attached garages. Every yard had maple and oak trees that looked like they had been there forever. In my mind, the families who lived in that neighborhood were the kind who ate together in the dining room and the kids probably had their own bedrooms. I bet kids didn't sleep in a converted basement like I had to at my aunt's house. This was the kind of suburban neighborhood that Doc was lucky to call home. Back then, I could only dream of living in a place like this.

Despite all of the hard work I was putting in with Doc, Coach Frost still wasn't rewarding me. My name wasn't on the travel list for the first two outdoor meets that spring. Not every track member traveled at the same time but I thought I would get on the travel list for at least the second meet. After the team returned from the second outdoor meet, I got up enough courage and went to Coach's office to see him. Coach Frost explained to me that I needed to try harder to make the team's practices. He was aware of my class schedule, but said it wasn't fair to the team if I traveled with them to the meets without practicing with the team. I then explained to him that I was in great shape and was ready to compete because I was doing extra training with Doc. With that, Coach Frost gave in just a little. He then said he would give me a shot at the Ball State Invitational in Indiana.

That was all I needed to hear. I worked hard over the next few weeks and I continued to train with Doc. Finally, the traveling list came out for the Ball State meet. I was on a travel team for the first time in two years. There were only a few of my old teammates from two years ago. One thing that I was glad of was that there was no Craig on the van talking bad about everyone. Even if Craig or someone like him was on the travel list, I was a different person than I was in 1978. I don't think Craig would have recognized the confident person I was becoming.

We arrived at the meet in Muncie, Indiana on a Friday and the long jump wasn't until Saturday morning. My past long jump partner, Dale, was no longer on the team and was deep into fraternity life as a member of Kappa Alpha Psi. During the warm-ups, I thought back to how poorly we did in our first track meet in freshman year. This time, I was hitting my mark perfectly on the board and was ready to jump.

There were flags in the sand pit just like a few years ago. I wasn't that worried about any markers because I was ready to compete. I jumped over 24 feet and won the meet. Just before the competition began I found a place where I could pray. I asked the Lord to guide me and keep me healthy during the competition. After the competition I knelt down and thanked God for his guidance. Like everything else those days, prayer had become easier for me. I no longer wondered why my grandmother seemed to say "thank you Jesus" about a dozen times a day.

The Ball State meet was a personal best for me and I qualified for the biggest competition of my life: the NCAA Division II Track & Field Championship in California. Coach Frost was so busy watching the other athletes that he never came over to see me jump. No one, including Coach Frost, had any idea how well I did until they announced the medal winners in the men's long jump. After they made the announcement I received my award. It was only a watch but it had me smiling from ear to ear. When I got back to the bleachers where most of the team was, I received plenty of congratulations. I was the only first place winner on the whole team. Coach Frost approached me and shook my hand and finally acknowledged that I could jump. He was starting to see me as a competitor and I had a feeling my relationship with him had changed. This definitely was not like the humiliating road trips from freshman year.

We got back to campus late Saturday evening. When I went to Doc's class on Monday and told him how I did, he was excited for me and agreed to work with me the next season if I wanted him to. Then he told me that he was going to retire at the end of the spring semester. I was shocked. How could he retire? I wasn't ready to graduate and there was a lot I needed to learn from him. It wasn't like I could talk with Coach Frost the way I could with Doc. He was the father I wished I had and soon, he was going to disappear, too.

I couldn't get Doc's news out of my mind. School had ended for the semester, which meant that Doc's office—which I could find blindfolded—was no longer his office. I flew home to Connecticut then went to Scranton. I played basketball with my old friends and pulled a hamstring in my right leg. After icing it for two days, my cousin, Larry, took me to see an athletic trainer at the University of Scranton. The trainer confirmed that it was a pulled hamstring.

With the championship meet only two weeks away, I wasn't going to be healthy enough to compete. I called Coach Frost, who said I had earned the trip to California and, as far as he was concerned, I was still going. I continued getting treatment from the trainer in Scranton who told me I needed a few weeks of treatment just to let it heal and probably a little longer before I could actually jump.

A few weeks later, I met Coach Frost in California. It was my first time on the west coast. The track and field championship was at California State Polytechnic University in Ponoma, about 30 miles east of downtown Los Angeles. Before I left to go home from the meet, we were out having dinner in a restaurant in Beverly Hills and I asked Coach Frost what I had to do to get a track scholarship for next year. He said that by making it to the national championships, there was nothing else I needed to do to earn it. If I wanted it, the track scholarship was mine. I felt incredible. I was grateful but Coach Frost was only able to see my success on the track. From my viewpoint, I could see all the ways I had faced hard times and come back, from the kid called Bubby whose pet turtle died to the teenager who experienced racism to the college student on the verge of flunking out. This track scholarship was a reward for persevering and a sign that, given the opportunity, I was capable of doing great things with my life.

◆ ◆ ◆ ◆ ◆ ◆ ◆ ◆ ◆ ◆ ◆

When you don't do your best, you know that you won't get any prizes. No one says "Good job!" when you fail. But when you work hard, when you do the very best you can, you expect the best to come your way. It's surprising to learn that life doesn't always work that way. Sometimes you put in the effort and you still don't get a chance to move ahead.

In those moments, maybe you feel that you deserve to be given a second chance or a third chance. Yet, second and third chances—even first chances—are best earned by showing that you are determined to be and to do your best. Stay focused. Show up. Be on time. Practice daily. Ask for help. If you want to be able to show the world what you can do, remember that:

Opportunity is Earned,
Not Given

CHAPTER NINE

H.E.L.P.—HEAR, ENCOURAGE, LOVE, AND PREPARE

The summer after the 1980 track and field championships made my confidence skyrocket. By winning first place in my division, I accomplished something that I set out to do and I didn't want to lose that feeling. Staying at school wasn't an option and I really wanted to see my grandparents, which is what I did at the beginning of summer and then it was back to Connecticut.

Throughout that summer I worked at a factory called Fafnir Bearing, one of the largest manufacturers of ball bearings in the country. There were other factories in New Britain, like the tool company Stanley Works, which produced everything from tools to small appliances; it's why New

Britain was called "Hardware City." There was plenty of work for everyone. My Uncle Curtis worked at Fafnir for more than 34 years, my late Uncle Erwin was there for 21 years and Aunt Thelma lasted 7 years. Even some of the people I went to high school with found work in the factories. For me, factory work was a summer job. At Fafnir, I worked for the food service department called ARA. I was what you call a wagon boy, going around the factory selling food to the factory employees. I never worked in the factory making anything but many of my friends' parents worked there. One of them was Mrs. Willis. I was friends with both of her sons, Mahrlon and Bryan. Every time I saw her she would tell me, "You don't want to work here and do this kind of work for the rest of your life." That stuck with me. Mrs. Willis didn't want me to end up like so many men in our community who made good money working for places like Fafnir but couldn't enjoy it because of the toll the intense physical labor took on their bodies. Her warning was never far from my mind that summer. I was even more determined to study hard for the rest of my time in college.

By the time I was relaxed and enjoying being out of school for the summer, it was time to return to Kentucky. The scholarship took care of tuition, which meant I could finally afford to live off campus. It wasn't like I spent most of my time at my apartment; I was taking six classes and studying, always studying. When I wasn't studying, I would hang out with Karl or I was going up to University of Kentucky to see Sam Bowie. Sam was like me and trained even if it wasn't the season for basketball. I'd watch him practice and we hung out in the Wildcat Lodge as much as we could.

A few weeks into the fall semester, Coach Frost announced that he was going to name me the captain of the track team. I was honored that he would think that I was capable of doing the job but I had to decline. I wasn't ready to handle that responsibility and my classes, too. Coach Frost said that he understood but I wondered if I would regret my decision once track season was here.

I also made time to see Dr. Exum. I had to visit him at his house because he had retired at the end of the spring semester. Although he wasn't my advisor anymore, I valued his opinions about the University's professors and I still asked him for advice on selecting my classes. Since I was a physical education major, I thought he was going to suggest that I take another science course. It was no secret to Doc that I struggled with science but he was an advocate of taking the tough road so that you could learn important lessons along the way. But he surprised me when he suggested that I take a Public Speaking class. If I was going to be a teacher I would have to be comfortable speaking in front of a class. But public speaking? Wasn't that about talking in front of crowds that were a lot larger than a classroom full of students? Doc said that one day I might become a public speaker and that I needed to start getting prepared early. I thanked him as politely as I could but, on the inside, I thought that Doc might be losing it. Even though I had no plans to ever be a public speaker, I ended up taking the public speaking class in the spring.

I saw Doc as much as I could. In the middle of September, I stopped back by Doc's house and he asked me how my classes and my training were going. I explained to him that I wasn't able to do any training because my schedule was full.

He paused for a minute, like he always did. He then asked, "What is your hardest class?"

"Anatomy and Physiology," I said. The class was a combination of a long, and sometimes, confusing lecture followed by a tough lab.

"You need to drop the class and concentrate on the other classes," Doc said. "By the way, you need to start training to get in shape before the official practice with the team starts."

As usual, Doc went from one topic to another, which barely gave me time to think. But it was a sure sign that retirement had not diminished his ability to offer the words of wisdom I needed.

While we were on the subject of track I asked if he would have the time to work with me again like last year and he said of course. I also told him that I declined Coach Frost's offer to be a track captain. Doc nodded his head and paused before he spoke again.

"Well, Mr. Shaw," he said, "it seems to me that you came to school to be a student not a track captain, so don't worry about it."

True to his word, Doc developed a workout schedule for me and I lived by it for the next few months. I took his advice and I dropped Anatomy and Physiology. I often saw Doc driving to his house on Mondays and Thursdays because those were the days that I was running up and down the hills on Cold Harbor Drive. He would roll his car window down and give me advice by yelling out the window.

"Lift your knees higher, Mr. Shaw!"

"Swing your arms!"

"Run faster!"

Before I could answer back he would speed off. Even if he wasn't driving by, I could hear him yelling instructions out to me. If I live to be 100, his is the voice I want to hear.

Track and classes kept me busy as usual that spring but I wanted to know more about fraternities. After my introduction to fraternity life in freshman year, I had learned more about black fraternities and sororities. My friends who belonged to them had a lot of fun and hosted the best parties. They all competed with one another but they respected each other, too.

Back home a few of my friends went to Morgan State University in Baltimore and they talked about a fraternity called Iota Phi Theta. Before the Iotas formed at Morgan State, they were active in demonstrations against segregation in Baltimore. The Iotas were all about community service and it was important to the 12 men who founded the fraternity in the 1960s to have a support organization for black male college students. If you asked anyone who was involved in black Greek life, they would talk about their organization's commitment to helping others, especially other black folks. There was so much that was positive about Iota. Karl felt the same way, too, and went with me to an interest meeting to learn more about them. Up until spring 1981, Iota did not have a presence on our campus but had received permission to start a charter line. After a long application process, Karl and I pledged during the spring semester. The only thing that was hard about pledging during those six weeks was that the Iota brothers made us go to mandatory study hall, which was after track practice. That took up a lot of my time. After pledging for 6 weeks, we went over, which means we became members of the fraternity, on May 2, 1981. Years later, Karl became the Grand Polaris, or national president, of Iota Phi Theta Fraternity, Inc.

Now, I was an athlete and an Iota. People looked at me as the track athlete and when they saw us in step shows, they were very surprised. I was a pretty low key person so they were shocked that I pledged anything. When I went to track meets during the next year I would run into other frat brothers from all over. And coming home was great because a lot of my friends that went away to school knew Iota brothers. I could now proudly wear Iota brown and gold.

The school year went by very fast and soon it was May of 1981. I had a great track season once again and broke several school records in indoor and outdoor track. The freshman class that I started with in 1977 was getting ready to graduate. Although I wasn't on schedule to graduate, it didn't bother me as much as I thought it would. I had been granted another year to run track by the NCAA because I wasn't a student athlete in my sophomore year. I wasn't going to graduate until next spring. It was still a sad time for me because Greg Harris, my friend over the last four years and the best person ever to come out of Chicago, was ready to walk across that stage. I loved him like one of my own brothers and would miss him a lot. While he was walking across that stage in

Kentucky, I was in New Britain training for the 1981 national championships.

The NCAA Division II Track and Field Championship took place at Western Illinois University in late May. Before Coach Frost and I left, I remember stopping by to see Doc.

"Mr. Shaw, it is your time to be added to the list," he said.

"What list?" I asked.

"The All-American list of Kentucky State's best track and field performers," he answered. "Last year you were injured and this year you are healthy. Go represent the school well and enjoy yourself!"

I don't know how he did it but Doc always made me feel better about my life. All I was doing was trying to be a really good athlete but Doc saw an amazing athlete. I could say thank you a million times a day and it wouldn't matter to Doc. He wanted me to continue to do well and I wasn't about to disappoint him.

Coach Frost and I stayed at the campus of Western Illinois University for six days. I trained very hard for four days and then I stopped. I never trained the day before competition. It's something I learned from Doc. He had a kind of a "1" and "3" rule: you don't need to practice if you walk a lot one day before your competition but you need at least three days to get mentally prepared. On both counts, I was as ready I was ever going to be.

The day of my event finally arrived. There were morning and evening events. That morning, I had three jumps to make in order to qualify for the evening round. I hit the mark on my first jump and headed back to my hotel with Coach Frost to rest for the evening.

Once the evening came it was time to head to the track. Every meet I went to, I would find someplace near the track where I could have a minute or two by myself. I thought about all of the hard work that I put in to get to this point. It was finally time to compete and I never felt better. Although the sun was about to set, the bright lights around the track made it look like it was the middle of the day. In the first round I made it to the finals by having one of the top 10 jumps. I was excited and confident. During the finals, you had to be in the top six in order to be named All-American. I finished in sixth place, which meant I was All-American.

After getting congratulations from Coach Frost, I went and prayed to thank the Lord for everything that he did to get me to that point. The feeling I had was unbelievable. I achieved something that a few years ago seemed impossible. This victory wasn't just mine; I shared it with three people who never left my side: my grandmother, Coach Black, and

Dr. Exum. I may have studied alone and trained alone but, with their love and encouragement, I was in good company.

◆ ◆ ◆ ◆ ◆ ◆ ◆ ◆ ◆ ◆ ◆

Sometimes you want to be around people who will agree with everything you do. They don't demand or expect anything of you. If you never changed, that would be okay. And then there are the people whose version of encouragement is to constantly tell you what to do. How can you feel encouraged when you're being told to try harder, to stop complaining, to do more than you did the day before?

In order to make positive changes, you need to be challenged by people who are not content with the person you have always been. Deep down you know that you can accomplish great things but that you can't do it alone. Find someone wiser than you, someone who will not let you settle, someone who will help you to become a better person. Believe that a good life is within your reach and that you deserve special people in your life who are willing to:

**H.E.L.P.—Hear, Encourage,
Love, and Prepare**

CHAPTER TEN

W.I.N.—WHAT'S IMPORTANT NOW

After the track and field championships at Western Illinois University, Coach Frost and I went back to Kentucky. He cautioned me against training too hard during the summer and encouraged me to take some time off. He knew me well; taking time off was something I rarely did. There were people from college who did nothing during the summer—no summer courses, no working out, no volunteering, not even a job. It just wasn't in me to do nothing at all with my time. No grandson of Madeline Williams was going to get caught doing nothing but hanging out during the summer. My grandmother couldn't see what I was doing in Connecticut, at least not from her house in Pennsylvania. But her words stayed with me. Coach Frost meant well but, for me, the summer meant that I switched gears but I stayed busy.

Before I left Kentucky for the summer, I stopped by Doc's house and showed him my All-American plaque. He was happy for me and told me that he never doubted my ability to succeed. We only talked a little about the meet and he explained to me that I had to win in another area just like I did on the track.

"Doc, what are you talking about?" I asked.

"When you return for the fall semester, you need to concentrate on graduating in the spring," he said. Although he wasn't really my advisor anymore, he was still telling me what classes I needed to take. He meant well but I didn't believe that he was right 100 percent of the time.

"Last semester you told me to take Public Speaking," I said. "It was the worst class I took because I didn't like speaking in front of my classmates. I ended up with a D in the class."

Doc nodded his head but he wasn't fazed by what I said. "Mr. Shaw, in the future you will look back at that class and wonder how you did so poorly in it."

I had worked so closely with Doc and I knew he believed in me but I didn't understand how he could be so positive about my future. Being a teacher was what I wanted to do but if Doc thought that public speaking would be important to my life, I wasn't going to argue with him.

After I got home everyone was excited for what I accomplished in Illinois, especially Aunt Thelma. I would hear her talking on the phone to her friends bragging about what I did in track. She was so excited for me that she took me out for a steak dinner. If Aunt Thelma spent her hard earned money, you must have done something good.

I also stopped by the high school track to see Coach Black. He wanted to know was how I was doing in school and when was I going to graduate. I said next May. In his typically stern way, he reminded me that I didn't go all the way to Kentucky to run track, that I was at Kentucky State University to get a good education and a college degree. He sounded just like he did when I ran for him at New Britain High School. Once a coach, always a coach.

I did my usual summer trip to Scranton to stay with my grandparents for two weeks. My grandmother's message was the same as Coach Black's: *I want to see you graduate.* The rest of the summer went well and was the same as it had been the past few years: working at the playground, training about three times a week, and running on the same track club with my friends.

Summer was over in a flash and it was time to return to Frankfort for my last year in college. I expected to feel different about school because so much was changing. Greg had graduated and was working in Chicago. I was still living off-campus but this time in a different apartment with two new roommates. What I didn't expect for my last year in college was a new track and field coach. Coach Frost didn't return to Kentucky. He took a new coaching job at another university. I was shocked and hurt at the same time because we had developed a great relationship over the past two years.

The new coach was Ron Moore, a very big guy with a great sense of humor. It was okay with him that I practiced alone and that I had help from Dr. Exum. Coach Moore didn't have a problem with my arrangement with Doc. Coach Moore trusted that I would be working out even when I wasn't with the team. Track continued to be rewarding and almost effortless; it really was the easiest part of my life. I told Coach Moore and anyone else who would listen that graduating in May was my main priority but there wasn't going to be anything easy or effortless in making that happen.

Before I registered for my fall semester classes, I had to see what classes I needed to take to be eligible for student teaching in the spring. In order for me to be a student teacher in the second semester, I had to take six classes and pass them all. Two of the classes were Anatomy & Physiology and Fundamentals of Math. I wasn't looking forward to taking either of those classes. I dropped Anatomy on three other occasions and I struggled just as bad in math. But if I didn't pass them, there wasn't going to be any student teaching next semester.

My math teacher, Mr. Devine, made everyone participate in class. As bad as I was in math, I just wanted to go to class and stay in my seat. But Mr. Devine required that all of us go up to the blackboard to solve math problems. I hated when he called on me because I usually needed help. One of my classmates, Sharon, seemed like a math genius to me; she never hesitated when it was her time to solve problems in front of the class.

One day after math class, Sharon said that I should let her know if I ever needed help with math. So about twice a week, we met in the student center and we would study for about 45 minutes. She was a great help to me. I gained a lot of confidence from her. I know that Mr. Devine noticed a difference in my work and I even worked up the courage to stop by his office a few times a week to get a better understanding of the work. My test scores were still low but he recognized that I was trying real hard to pass his class. I made it through the final exam and Fundamentals of Math with a D, which meant I could begin student teaching in the spring. Getting a D in a class isn't something I would have bragged about but that day was one of the happiest days of my life. I accomplished a lot because it was something that I was determined to do. I wondered if my attitude about math was affecting my other classes because Anatomy & Physiology was a little easier this time around and with a lot of studying, I finally passed that class, too. I had one semester to go and, if I passed every class in the spring, I would graduate in May.

My practice sessions went well for the most part. I did mostly strength training in the weight room and a lot of bounding drills up the stadium stairs. I would stop by Doc's house to get workouts from him but it was clear that Doc wasn't himself for most of that fall. Most days that I would go up to visit him, his wife would answer the door and say that he wasn't feeling well.

After a while, I kind of got the message that his illness was a bit more serious than I thought. After weeks of not seeing him, one day his wife let me in to see him. He had lost a lot of weight and he wasn't talkative like he used to be. He was having some health issues and after that one visit I didn't return to see him again until the spring semester.

My last semester of college, I was running on three different roads: track, classes, and student teaching. Of the three, track was the most natural thing to me. I wondered if anything in my life would ever feel as comfortable to me as track. Even though I had one semester to go, I was already starting to miss track and school and everything that KSU meant to me.

I had plenty of time before school was over and it was important for me to stay focused. Practicing alone was all I usually needed but that semester I started practicing with one of my good friends. His name was Rod Hill but we called him "Pub" for short. That nickname stood for publicity. He was a very funny guy who liked to tell jokes but when it came to practicing, he was serious. My plate had been so full with classes and track that I didn't have any time to hang out with my friends. Working out with Pub made up for some of that.

Pub, who was from Detroit, was a unbelievable cornerback on the KSU football team. He was getting ready for the National Football League Combine, which was when they brought together the most talented players from across the country and tested them in front of NFL coaches and scouts. We worked out for a few weeks together. We would lift weights and then run. Pub knew that I trained alone. I didn't mind working out with him because—besides all of the jokes and storytelling—he was a very gifted athlete. He helped me improve my speed because he was so explosive from the start. Every day that we trained it was like a job. After about four weeks of training, he went to the NFL Combine and astonished everyone with his ability. I was so happy for him because he accomplished what he wanted to. Next up for him was the NFL draft in April. I was a big Dallas Cowboy fan and I had hoped that Pub might get drafted by them. The Dallas Cowboys selected him in the first round with the 25th pick. It was unbelievable. I was calling home telling everyone that Rod Hill, the newest Dallas Cowboy, was one of my friends. It was nice to feel good for someone else's success and it kept my mind off of the thing I was dreading: student teaching.

I only had two classes that semester, Methods of Teaching Physical Education and the second part of Anatomy & Physiology. The bulk of my time was dedicated to my student teaching class, which was broken up into two 8-week segments. The hardest part of the class was teaching in an actual school for eight weeks. The advisor and teacher was Ms. Juanita Wright. She was very tough on me and I never understood why. After the eight weeks in the classroom, it was time to go to our assigned schools. I was assigned to Lexington Junior High School in Lexington, KY. I had money for gas but did not have a car. Ms. Wright paired me up with another student teacher, Terry Jackson, who had a car. I had known Terry for about three years and we were pretty good friends. She picked me up every day and at the end of every week, I gave her gas money.

I was assigned to teach physical education. When I was a kid, gym was everyone's favorite class because it was fun. It didn't take me long to learn that gym is a lot harder and not as much fun when you're the teacher. The students at the junior high were loud and energetic one minute, then quiet and moody the next. Some were athletes and a lot of them were very smart. I tried to apply what I learned in class that semester but also discovered that I could deal with these kids the same way I handled the kids during my summer job. As far as I was concerned, student teaching was going okay.

Terry and I knew that Ms. Wright had to observe our teaching. Ms. Wright showed up for the first time to observe Terry and me during the second week. After staying for about 45 minutes Ms. Wright told me to stop by her office at 4:00pm. When I went to see her she gave me a lecture that I never had before in my life. She said that I had little control of the class and that my voice wasn't loud enough. "Your voice," she said, "has to be used as a weapon of control." The last thing she said was that she would be back in a few weeks and that I better show her some improvement.

Maybe I should have worried about what Ms. Wright said but I didn't. My mind was on the next big meet, which was at Indiana University.

That meet was more than I could hope for. I placed 3rd in the meet and lost to the Big Ten long jump champion. The next weekend I was heading to the University of Tennessee in Knoxville, TN. Some of the best jumpers in the country were at that meet. I had a great week of training and was very excited to see where I stood with the best jumpers in the SEC conference. I didn't jump until Saturday afternoon. It was the best competition field that I had ever jumped against. I jumped the best I ever jumped and finished 4th. After hearing my name called over the loud speaker, I picked up my medal and was stopped by a man who told me that he was proud to see that I was jumping well. It was Coach Gibson, the man that kicked me off the team during my freshman year. I was impressed with the fact that he still remembered who I was. I still felt bitter about what he did to me years ago but at least he finally saw me as a skilled and confident athlete.

Later that spring, Kentucky State University honored all of the school teams and their outstanding athletes. I was named the outstanding athlete of the track team. The biggest award was given to the KSU's most outstanding athlete. Everyone thought that Pub was going to get it, especially after he got drafted in the first round by a professional football team. Well, to my surprise, I was given that award. It was the biggest honor from KSU that I had ever received. I worked hard at school and track and tried to be a respectable person. I could never ever have dreamed of winning such an award.

Maybe that's why I was so humble and happy and hopeful that more good things could come my way.

It was finally time for Ms. Wright to visit my classroom at Lexington Junior High School again for the fourth and final time. The second and third times she observed my teaching left me confused because each time she said that I had shown some improvement. But I needed more than "some improvement." I only had one opportunity for student teaching. This visit was extremely important because if I didn't get her approval then I was not going to pass the class. And if I did not pass, I would not graduate.

After Ms. Wright observed my class, Terry drove me back to campus. I was so quiet on the way back that Terry thought something was wrong. My teaching career hadn't really started and it could be taken away if my meeting with Ms. Wright did not go well.

I went directly to Ms. Wright's office once Terry dropped me off.

As I sat in the chair across from Ms. Wright, I crossed everything—my hands, toes, legs and whatever else I could. I also prayed a lot for the Lord to be with me as he had whenever I was in difficult situations. Ms. Wright started off by saying that she was impressed with what she saw over the eight weeks.

"Your classes were well behaved every time I came to see you," she said. "The students were always aware of who was in control. Mr. Shaw, one day you are going to make a fine teacher for some school district."

Me? A fine teacher? I was stunned. I thought she hated me and was sure that my teaching career was never going to happen if Ms. Wright had her way. After she spoke, she asked me if I had any questions for her.

"Why did you tell me that I wasn't doing a good job every time I came to see you?" I asked.

She paused and told me something I never thought I would hear from her.

"You were this big track star on campus. I didn't want you to think that you were going to just slide by and pass the class without putting in the necessary work like all of the other students," she confessed. "You were never doing anything wrong."

At first I wanted to tell her off because she had me under stress for eight weeks. But how was this different than what I heard from every coach I ever had? It wasn't. In fact, it was almost the same. I realized the messages she had been sending to me throughout the semester: *Never, ever stay satisfied with anything because of your status. Strive to improve no matter the situation.* In that small office, I was beginning to feel that it was possible that I could be a decent teacher if only I looked at failure as an opportunity to become better.

With only a few weeks left in the semester, it was time for another big meet: the Kentucky Relays. I didn't have the stress anymore from my student teaching because it was over and I was doing very well in my Anatomy & Physiology class.

I jumped 25 feet and 9 ½ inches and won the event. Although I had a personal best—it was the 19th best in the United States that year—I only took two jumps because I strained my left hamstring while attempting my third jump. I wanted to go for 26 feet so bad. But I remembered a few years ago when I pulled my hamstring in Scranton while playing basketball. I had a few more big meets ahead of me and I needed to rest. Almost 26 feet would have to be good enough.

Back on campus, final exams were somewhat of a sad time for me. The friendships that I had developed throughout the years were about to come to an end because I had no idea if or when I would see my friends again. I stopped by to see the man who helped me to become the best person and athlete that I became—Dr. Exum. I thanked him for all of his wisdom and inspiring words over the years.

"Doc," I said. "You are my angel that God had put in my life."

With his soft voice, he said, "I want you to do three things, Mr. Shaw. First, I want you to walk across the stage on graduation day and remember how hard it was to accomplish that moment. Number two, go to California and repeat as an All-American in the long jump and remember how your track career began."

Doc paused before revealing his final request. "Go back to New Britain, Mr. Shaw, and help some of the students realize and understand that the world is full of opportunities. Tell them that they need to find opportunities to make their lives worth living."

When I left his home on my short walk back to my apartment I felt like I would never see him again.

The end of the semester brought a close to my college athletic career. How could five years go so fast? It seemed like a minute ago I was a 17 year old who had just taken his first plane ride on the way to a college he never knew existed. Now, I was 22, a well-respected athlete about to represent his college again at the NCAA Division II Track and Field Championships in Sacramento, CA.

I flew out to Sacramento with Coach Moore and four members of the KSU track and field team, as well as my frat brother, Karl Price, the one and only KP. I was the lead off leg for the 4x100 meter relay team but a registration error disqualified our team so we were unable to run. I still had the long jump to look forward to. Like so many meets before, you had to qualify for the long jump in the morning to make it to the next round that same night. I qualified on my first jump.

That evening, it finally hit me that this was the last time that I would be representing my university. I jumped 24 feet and 10 inches, which wasn't my best but I placed 4th and repeated as an All-American in the long jump. I became Kentucky State University's first two-time All-American in the long jump. When I took my place on the podium for the awards ceremony, I felt a kind of joy and pride that I will remember for the rest of my life. Never in my wildest dreams did I think I would have such a great college track career and be recognized as one of the best track athletes to ever come out of Kentucky State University. All of the hard work paid off.

While Sacramento was an amazing experience, nothing matched what I was feeling as graduation neared. I could have touched the sky in one jump. No one ever saw me without a smile on my face. But there were brief moments when I wished my mother could have lived to see the young man I turned into. I had to believe that she was looking out for me wherever she was and that she was sending me her love and support. I carried that thought with me as I prepared to leave college behind.

The day before graduation, Coach Moore asked me to take a ride with him. I jumped in his car and we arrived at a Holiday Inn that was a few miles away from the campus. He said he needed to see someone for a few minutes but I didn't have to wait in the car. Coach Moore knocked on a hotel room door and, to my surprise, my Aunt Thelma opened the door. I remember grabbing and hugging her.

"We wouldn't miss seeing you graduate if it was the end of the world!" she said.

"Who is *we?*" I asked and Aunt Thelma told me to go inside the room. Sitting in a chair was my grandmother. I hugged her and tears started rolling down my face. I was so happy to see them. Coach Moore had arranged for them to attend my graduation. We had a great few days together. In a strange but wonderful way my entire life was in one room: the Kentucky college student, the Connecticut teenager, and the kid from Pennsylvania. I couldn't have asked for a better graduation present.

The next day was the biggest day of my life. I was about to get rewarded for all of my hard work in the classrooms over the past five years. As I sat in the audience at the Capital Plaza Civic Center in Frankfort, KY, I realized that my dream of being a college graduate was about to become a reality. The degrees were handed out alphabetically by last name. Since my last name started with an *S*, I had to wait a while. And while I waited, I had time to think about the great people who helped me obtain this moment. Mainly I thought of Coach Black for giving me an opportunity to meet a great man like Dr. Exum. Without those two, none of this would have been possible. I thought about the great instructors and friends that I made over the years. As I watched the glow on my grandmother's and Aunt Thelma's faces sitting in the audience, I couldn't help to think what my life would be like without them. Aunt Thelma and I had not always seen eye to eye but she had given me a roof over my head and a reason to think about the kind of parent I wanted to be someday. Those early years with her were tough but it built in me a determination to endure. My grandmother, however, was a different story. She meant everything to me from the day I was born. Her love and faith guided me throughout my life and she is the first angel God sent my way. After they called my name and I walked across that stage to receive my college degree, the weight of all of the hard work escaped my body. I had earned something that no one could take away. I wish I could have written Coach Black, Dr. Exum, and Madeline Williams on my degree because it really belonged to them as much as it belonged to me.

Sometimes success is so near you can touch it. It feels like victory will come to you even if the task is not complete. After all, you've done the hard work and resting is your reward. This is when we often lose instead of win. If you rest on your past achievements, you'll be settling for an *okay* life instead of an *outstanding* life.

The most important step is the step you are about to take. Every stage of your life will present different challenges for you to conquer. That's okay. You have what you need to be extraordinary. Keep moving. Keep striving. Keep running while there is still a race to be run. To achieve everything you are destined to have, everything you are meant to enjoy, you have to focus on:

W.I.N.—
What's Important Now

ACKNOWLEDGMENTS

From Darwin F. Shaw:

Thank you God, I give you all the honor and glory for giving me life, and for being my best friend in the whole wide world who has been with me through all of the good and bad times throughout my life. Each and every day that I call on you, you have been there and continue to answer my call. I love you with all of my heart and soul.

To my mother, Carolyn Mae Shaw, thank you for all you did for me for the short time that you were in my life. You had a very tough life and you sacrificed everything to provide for me, Dawn, Early and Jeffrey. You were a great mom and I will always love you from the bottom of my heart.

My sister Dawn, and brothers, Jeffrey and Early. No one will ever know all of the things that we encountered during our childhood. But the Lord made sure that he stood by us and fought all of the evil things that came our way and helped us to survive. I love all of you so much.

Grandparents, Mr. & Mrs. Francis Williams, there aren't enough words to describe what I feel for you. Grandma, you always told me that God was my best friend and whenever I needed him all I had to do was call on him and he would be there. When the world was caving in on me, I always remembered those words. I called on Him then and I am still calling. I love and miss you both so much. Thank you, for helping me become the person that I am today.

Coach Irving Black, thanks for giving me the opportunity to go away to college at Kentucky State University and believing in me. Without you in my life, I don't know where I would have ended up.

Dr. William Exum, you described to me what my life was going to be like the first time I met you. Attending Kentucky State University was one of the best experiences of my life. You were everything that I needed out of a mentor. You were the dad that I never had. All I want to say is thank you for being there and treating me like your son.

Renee Hamilton Jones, thank you for being my girlfriend as well as my best friend. You encouraged me so much to do this project. Without your motivation and drive, this book wouldn't have happen. I love you enormously.

Kerry L. Beckford, thank you so much for taking on this project. You have been an inspiration for me throughout this whole project. There aren't any words to describe what you mean to me. Your dedication cannot be measured and I hope the whole world can see how incredible a writer you are. I love you dearly and may God continue to bless you.

A special thanks to, uncles Curtis and Erwin Williams, aunts Edna "Skee" Williams and Thelma Santiago Phillips, cousins Lori Coe and Lisa, Toby and Darryl Williams. Thanks also go to Jeff Gambino, Scott Skates, Robin Shaw, Annie Parker, Michael "Chief" Peterson, Jessica Thomas Bryant, Lisa Frazier Page, Stan Simpson, William Bumpus, Patricia Mitchell, Mrs. Juanita Wright, Larry Conaway, Carl Dean, Dinky McCloe, Geneva Ivy, Pastor John C. Morris Jr., Mr. and Mrs. Albert Vieira, and Charlotte Owens Price.

To all the friends, co-workers, students and athletes who I have known throughout the years, I am grateful for your encouragement and for your belief in this project.

And most of all, to my son, Garrett, and daughters, Porcia and Myia, and grandson, Julian. I want to say that all of you are my inspiration and why I live each and every day. I hope that you understand that the things I do are for all of you. I hope that you look at me as your hero, because you are mine. I love you more then you will ever know. You are my heart.

From Kerry L. Beckford:

Thank you, Darwin, for your boundless faith in my writing and for your undying friendship. When you told me that you wanted to write a book, I thought it was a great idea. When you later asked me to co-author the book with you, I realized you trusted me with your dream to tell your life story. It is one thing to be a writer who is able to tell her own story. It is another thing to craft someone else's story and to treat that story with the utmost care and respect. I hope I have done this book justice.

I am grateful to all those who read early versions of this book and who provided gentle—yet firm!—suggestions along the way.

S. Edward Weinswig, thank you for providing such meticulous editing. You are a treasure, my friend.

Linda Alcorace, many thanks for your feedback on the narrative flow; your priceless advice is only surpassed by your own amazing writing and your deep compassion for humanity.

To writing friends Faye Rapoport DesPres and Angela Foster, thanks for holding my hand during the early stages of writing this book. Your guidance is always well timed and greatly appreciated.

To Don Jones, Beth Richards, Cindy Zelman, Rev. Tamara Moreland, Lisa Frazier Page, and Stan Simpson—I am deeply indebted to you for your support. It means the world to me.

To my sister, Kimberly Beckford, a million thank you's for your creative skills. The artist in you was indispensable to the cover design and promotional materials.

Finally, to my mother, Gloria J. Beckford—thanks for encouraging me to use the gifts God gave me, for understanding my need to create, and for always giving me space for my writing to grow.

About the Authors

Darwin F. Shaw has been a teacher and coach at his alma mater, New Britain High School, since 1985. He teaches physical education and coaches boys' junior varsity basketball and is the head coach for the girls' outdoor track & field team. He is also an entrepreneur ("Coach Shaw's Famous Sweet Potato Pies"), motivational speaker, and director of the Osgood Shootout, an annual basketball tournament whose proceeds help to fund college scholarships to graduates of New Britain High School.

Darwin earned a bachelor's degree in physical education from Kentucky State University, where he set several athletic records and was an NCAA All-American in 1981 and 1982. He holds a master's degree in psychology from Springfield College. Darwin was inducted into the Kentucky State University Athletic Hall of Fame and was recognized by the NAACP for his outstanding contributions to the community. He was selected as the Connecticut High School Boys Assistant Basketball Coach of the Year and is a member of Iota Phi Theta Fraternity, Inc. Darwin is also the recipient of several community service awards.

Darwin lives in New Britain, Connecticut and can be reached at becomingcoachshaw@gmail.com.

❧

Kerry L. Beckford is a nonfiction writer and teacher. Kerry has taught college composition, rhetoric, and communication for almost two decades. She is the co-author, with Donald C. Jones, of *Connections: An Integrated Reader and Rhetoric for College Writing* (Kendall Hunt Publishing, 2015).

Kerry holds a bachelor's degree and a master's degree in communication from University of Hartford and a master of fine arts degree in creative nonfiction from The Solstice Low-Residency MFA in Creative Writing Program at Pine Manor

College. Kerry's nonfiction work has appeared in, among others, Northeast Magazine, Connotation Press: An Online Artifact, The Hog River Journal, and The Hartford Courant. Kerry is writing a memoir about her American and Caribbean roots and is an avid essayist. She blogs at "This is Who I Am" at www.kerrybeckford.com.

A native New Englander, Kerry resides in central Connecticut.

Made in the USA
San Bernardino, CA
08 October 2014